D1384292

CONTROVERSY!

Health Care:

A Right or a Privilege?

Corinne J. Naden

Marshall Cavendish
Benchmark
New York

Marshall Cavendish Benchmark
99 White Plains Road
Tarrytown, NY 10591
www.marshallcavendish.us

Library of Congress Cataloging-in-Publication Data

Naden, Corinne J.
Health care : a right or a privilege? / by Corinne J. Naden.
p. cm.—(Controversy!)
Includes bibliographical references and index.
ISBN 978-0-7614-4231-8
1. Medical policy—United States—Juvenile literature.
2. Right to health care—United States—Juvenile literature. I. Title.
RA395.A3N2855 2010
362.1—dc22
2008047190

Publisher: Michelle Bisson
Art Director: Anahid Hamparian
Series Designer: Alicia Mikles

Photo research by Lindsay Aveilhe and Linda Sykes Picture Research, Inc., Hilton Head, SC

Cover photo: Julie Nicholls/Corbis

The photographs in this book are used by permission and through the courtesy of:
Ed Kashi/Corbis: 4, 72; Richard Perry/<I>New York Times<I>/Redux: 11;
Paul Kuroda/Alamy: 15; Alex Wong/Getty Images: 24; Adrianna Williams/zefa/Corbis: 31;
www.krankycartoons.com: 35; George Mattei/Photo Researchers, Inc.: 39;
Bettmann/Corbis: 51, 58; Reuters/Corbis: 64; Anthony Bolante/Reuters/Corbis: 67;
Monica Almeida/New York Times/Redux: 75; Mark A. Johnson/Corbis: 79;
Hulton Archive/Getty Images: 83; 20th Century Fox/The Kobal Collection: 86;
Robert Galbraith/Reuters: 90; AP Images: 93; James Estrin/New York Times/Redux: 107;
Ruby Washington/New York Times/Redux: 111; Rick Friedman/Corbis: 113.

Printed in Malaysia
1 3 5 6 4 2

Contents

As the rolls of the uninsured grew in the early twenty-first-century United States, a few free health clinics—such as this one in Homestead, Florida—opened their doors.

Introduction

WHY DOESN'T SOMEBODY DO SOMETHING? THAT'S
what many people ask about the health-care system in the United
States. It needs fixing, they say. But who can fix it? And how?

For years, politicians and insurance companies have boasted that
U.S. health care is the best in the world. But is that true? It's a fact
that millions of Americans are without health-care insurance at all. It's
a fact that the United States has one of the highest infant mortality
rates among all industrialized nations: 6.8 deaths per 1,000 births
compared to 3 in Japan and Sweden, and 4 in France and Germany.
(Lack of access to health facilities is often cited as one reason for
the high figure.) It's a fact that many Americans who are covered by
health insurance can't afford to pay for the prescription drugs they
need. And it's a fact that many Americans don't give high marks to
their health care. They say it is not the best medical system in the
world; it's just the most expensive.

Critics of the system also point out that the United States is the
only major country in the world that does not look upon health care
as a major right of its citizens. Instead, it is a service or commodity to
be purchased by consumers.

On the other hand, many other Americans think the U.S. system
is the best in the world. They say the quality of U.S. health care is
better than in other countries. They point out that waiting times to
see specialists or enter a hospital are shorter than almost anywhere
else. They cite the availability of medicines and the ongoing medical

research that brings new cures and new methods of treatment to thousands of patients.

A survey by the Harvard School of Public Health (HSPH) called *Debating Health: Election 2008* found that Americans are split over the merits of the health-care system with a significant divide along party lines. According to the survey: Nearly seven-in-ten Republicans (68%) believe the U.S. health-care system is the best in the world, compared to just three in ten (32%) Democrats and four in ten (40%) Independents who feel the same way. The World Health Organization (WHO), an agency of the United Nations, ranks the U.S. health-care system number thirty-seven in the world. However, during his administration, President George W. Bush often asserted that it is the best in the world. So have other prominent politicians. Even so, these people concede that the system could work better. They talk of tax rebates and a cap on medical malpractice suits as possible ways of insuring a more efficient, workable system.

If the system should be changed, how should it be done? Is a complete overhaul the answer, changing to a system such as in Canada or Great Britain? Or should the changes come in small steps, as has been the current solution, applying Band-Aids that tend to make access even more confusing. An example is the addition of Medicare plan D coverage for drugs, with multiple choices that baffle most senior citizens. Any change will be challenging given the track record of drug and insurance companies who want to keep in place a system that has been working for them.

In the face of all these possibilities, let us take an overall look at health care in the United States, its strengths, its regulations, and its inefficiencies. How does the U.S. health-care system compare with other countries around the world? If it is really good, can we make it better? And if there really is a mess, how can we fix it?

1 Who Provides Health Care?

Fact: The United States is . . . the only industrialized country that does not guarantee health insurance to its citizens through a national health insurance system.
—Connecticut Coalition for Universal Health Care, 2008

HEALTH CARE IN THE UNITED STATES IS A CRAZY quilt of different medical plans and services. An American who needs medical attention or coverage faces a bewildering list of people, institutions, organizations, plans, and practices. There are primary care physicians, hospitals and hospices; nursing homes and home health-care programs; drug companies and insurance companies; ambulatory care sites; and managed-care plans. There are also Medicare and Medicaid. Read on as these areas are defined and explored.

Even with this crazy quilt, America, unlike most major industrialized nations, does not guarantee health care to all its citizens. Most Germans have been covered by a health-care system since the 1880s. Great Britain adopted the National Health Service (NHS) in 1948, the world's first government-provided universal system. Canada has universal health care; so do Brazil, Costa Rica, India, Japan, and Cuba, among others.

According to the *U.S. News & World Report,* in 2008, "The percentage of Americans without health insurance rose to 15.8 percent in 2006 from 15.3 in 2005." (That percentage means

A Quick Look at Some Health-care Terms

AMBULATORY-CARE SITE: facility such as a doctor's office for outpatient treatment

CLINIC: health facility providing outpatient care

DRUG COMPANY OR PHARMACEUTICAL COMPANY: a commercial business that researches, develops, and markets health-care drugs

HEALTH INSURANCE: plan that covers medical expenses and may include disabilities and long-term nursing. The Franklin Health Assurance Company of Massachusetts was the first to offer accident insurance in the United States in 1850; it covered injuries from railroad and steamboat mishaps.

HEALTH INSURANCE COMPANY: business that offers health-care insurance coverage

HOME HEALTH-CARE PROGRAM: plan for individuals to receive health services at home

HOSPITAL: usually a large facility that treats various medical problems, some on an outpatient basis, but most inpatient

INPATIENT: Receiving lodging and food as well as medical treatment

MANAGED-CARE PLAN: private system that controls financing and delivery of health services to members of the plan

MEDICAID: U.S. government health-care program for low-income persons

MEDICARE: U.S. government health-care program for those sixty-five or older and people under sixty-five with special problems such as Lou Gehrig's disease or advanced kidney failure

NURSING HOME: facility for those who need special or constant health care

OUTPATIENT TREATMENT: medical care not requiring an overnight hospital stay

PRENATAL CLINIC: facility, often for low-income patients, providing care and information for expectant parents

PRIMARY-CARE PHYSICIAN: usually the doctor a person sees for basic medical needs

URGENT-CARE CENTER: generally a walk-in clinic for medical problems not requiring hospitalization, such as a badly sprained ankle or a reaction to a bee sting more than 47 million Americans had no health insurance in 2006.) According to the U.S. Census Bureau, in 2006: "In the United States, around 84% of citizens have some form of health insurance; either through their employer (60%), purchased individually (9%), or provided by government programs (27%); there is some overlap in these figures." Government programs account for more than 45 percent of all health-care spending in the United States, making the government the nation's largest insurer. That is largely because the government insures the elder population through Medicare, and that is the group with the highest rate of medical usage.

Outpatient Care

Most health care in the United States takes place on an outpatient basis—mainly in a doctor's office or clinic. Most Americans who are covered by health insurance go to a primary-care physician (PCP), also called a general practitioner (GP), for basic health needs. The doctor may refer the patient to a specialist, such as a gastroenterologist (who treats digestive organs) or a cardiologist (heart specialist). Some health plans allow the patient to go directly to a specialist. In some regions, often in rural areas or inner cities, the patient may see a health provider who is not a physician, but is qualified as a nurse practitioner or physician's assistant. Depending on their level of education, these health-care providers can treat illnesses, prescribe medicines, and even perform some minor surgeries.

Many medical procedures don't require a hospital visit. Ambulatory care, which means that treatment is given on an outpatient basis, is fine for such things as X rays or blood tests. The patient goes to the doctor's office, which is the most common site for ambulatory care. For some procedures, such as the setting of a broken arm, a patient may receive ambulatory care in a hospital.

Sometimes people—often those without health insurance— go to hospital emergency departments for what turns out to be

Walk-In MEDICAL CARE

Medical Services Provided By Paul James Endres MD, P.C.

Open 7 Days a Week!

In many parts of the country, there are not enough primary-care physicians to meet the needs of the community. As a result, walk-in clinics in drugstores and big chain stores are becoming a big business.

ambulatory care. They may complain of a fever or severe rash, for instance. Although some emergency room visits do require admission to the hospital, most do not.

Some patients receive ambulatory treatment in urgent-care centers. These centers are designed to treat ailments not severe enough for hospital admission. However, some patients may need to be treated quickly or at times when the doctor's office is closed. For instance, a patient may visit an urgent-care center in the early morning hours complaining of a severe earache.

In addition to these medical institutions, ambulatory care is available for students in their schools and for inmates in U.S. prisons. Visits to the dentist, eye doctor, or dermatologist (skin specialist) are also usually on an ambulatory care basis.

A new and somewhat controversial concept in personal health care arose in the late 1990s. It is generally called concierge, boutique, or retainer medicine. It means that a consumer gets personal care and attention from a primary-care physician. For instance, if a concierge patient gets the flu, his or her doctor may make a home visit instead of the patient going to the doctor's office. The patient may have twenty-four-hour-a-day access to the doctor, including the doctor's cell phone number, which is not generally the case in most doctor-patient relationships. And the concierge patient never has to wait in a crowded reception room.

All this service is not cheap; in fact, it is primarily available only to the wealthy. For example, a concierge patient may pay a $2,000 yearly fee, and some fees are much higher. That is in addition to the amount he or she may pay for an office appointment, billed to insurance. And then there are Medicare premiums or copays (the patient pays a portion of the charge) for special services. Some concierge doctors don't take insurance.

Not very many U.S. physicians offer this kind of care so far, although there are boutique doctors from New York to California. One drawback is that it limits the number of patients a doctor can see. Some doctors give regular as well as concierge care. That may seem like stretching a doctor's time very thin. But the American Medical Association (AMA) says that this medical trend does not violate medical ethics as long as "those paying such an extra fee and those who are not . . . get an equal quality of care from that practitioner."

In some areas of the country, pharmacies, for instance, are hiring health providers such as nurse practitioners. These health-care workers make periodic visits to the store to see patients with medical problems rather than going to a medical facility. Sometimes a doctor schedules health-care services that, in addition to skilled nurses, involve social workers, health aides, and physical, speech, or occupational therapists. These people may work in hospitals, clinics, offices, or the patient's home.

Social workers help people with problems. They might counsel a family with a gravely ill member about care options. They might try to find shelter for a homeless person. Child, family, and school social workers may find foster homes for abused or homeless children.

Medical and public health social workers advise people who have longtime health problems. Mental health and substance abuse social workers counsel those with mental illness or alcohol abuse.

Personal and home health-care aides help the elderly, physically disabled, and mentally disabled. They work in the patients' homes or in health-care facilities and institutions. They may work in one home for months or even longer, and their duties vary according to need. These aides generally work on their own with periodic visits from a supervisor, who may be a registered nurse, physical therapist, or social worker.

Physical therapists help people with limited or permanent disability caused by injury or disease. Treatment generally involves some type of exercise as well as electrical stimulation to relieve pain. Speech therapy is a painstaking process. A speech therapist works with those who have difficulty speaking, perhaps resulting from a brain injury, or those who stutter. The occupational therapist works with patients who suffer from a physically or developmentally disabling condition, such as spinal cord injury or muscular dystrophy. Their main aim is for the patient to be able to care for his or her daily needs.

Hospital Care

Hospitals are generally large institutions that treat patients with medical problems that can't be treated in a doctor's office, such as heart surgery. Besides surgeries, patients may go to the hospital for childbirth, a bad drug reaction, or an automobile accident injury. The two main types of hospitals in the United States are nonprofit and for-profit.

Most U.S. hospitals are nonprofit. That means they are organized like any nonprofit organization: they must serve some public purpose, which allows them special treatment under the law such as property tax and income tax exemptions. Despite the name, nonprofit hospitals can make a profit (and many do); they just can't be designed primarily for that purpose. Some nonprofit hospitals have ties to a religious institution, such as New York–Presbyterian Hospital in New York City. They may be governed by religious leaders or run by, for instance, nuns of the Sisters of Charity or other religious order.

A for-profit hospital is usually operated by a private corporation. Unlike the nonprofit sector, these investor-owned institutions, which increased in the late twentieth century, are set up to bring in a profit for their shareholders. They claim that with their emphasis on high efficiency, they can offer better care at lower cost than the nonprofit sector. Hospital Corporation of America (formerly Columbia/HCA) is the largest of this type. It is based in Nashville, Tennessee, and runs about 170 hospitals in twenty U.S. states and in London, England.

Detractors of for-profit hospitals say they are successful because they mainly serve the wealthy and avoid areas that would have to treat a largely poor population. They claim that these institutions specialize in such expensive procedures as elective plastic surgery and avoid unprofitable services like emergency medicine, which tends to treat the poor or those without insurance.

Probably the busiest place in a hospital is the emergency room (ER). People go to the ER for a sudden medical emergency, such as a heart attack or a severe allergic reaction to an insect bite. They go to the ER with a medical symptom if they are in a strange town and cannot reach their own physician. They visit the ER if they are uninsured. The emergency room at any hospital is usually clearly identified by a prominent sign, often white lettering on a red background.

Actually, the term *emergency room* is a misnomer. The modern hospital may have several rooms or areas to be used for emergency cases. The first stop in an emergency room is usually the triage area. *Triage* is a French word meaning "to sort," which is what the triage nurse does. He or she sorts out the order in which patients will

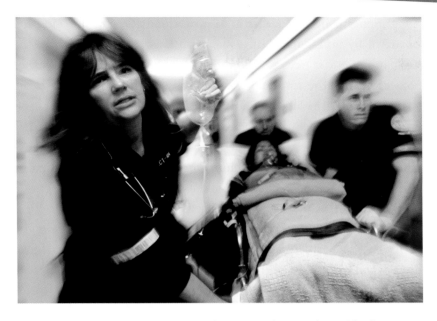

Emergency rooms are meant to take care of just that—life-threatening emergencies—but they have become the place of first resort to many of the uninsured, and even to those who have insurance but don't have access to their doctors when they are ill or injured.

be seen, depending on the seriousness of the condition. A badly sprained ankle can wait, but a compound fracture of the leg may require a doctor's attention right away. After triage, the patient may be sent to the general medical area where people with all sorts of problems await a further look, or may even be admitted to the hospital. They may be confined to bed in the area, which is generally a gurney—a cot on wheels—rather than a hospital bed. Another key ER site is the resuscitation area. It contains oxygen tubes, defibrillator equipment to restore normal heart rhythms, and emergency drugs to regulate the heartbeat. Some ERs have a pediatric area for children. However, if a pregnant woman visits the ER, she will probably be sent directly to the hospital's obstetrics/maternity ward. Some ERs may also have a separate area for patients with psychiatric problems.

Patients generally either transport themselves to the hospital or arrive by ambulance. After being seen by the triage nurse, the walk-in patient is treated according to the seriousness of his or her condition, not the time of arrival. However, those who get to the ER by ambulance will probably be taken directly to the resuscitation area. With a seriously ill patient, the ambulance crew notifies the ER that they are on the way and reports on what they think is wrong. The patient may be met by a trauma team, which consists of doctors and nurses and, if necessary, a surgeon and anesthesiologist.

Probably the biggest problem facing ERs in the United States, as well as in most other countries, is overcrowding. Increasingly, people use the ER for nonemergency services. A man may injure his arm on a Sunday afternoon when his doctor's office is closed. He fears it may be broken, so he goes to the emergency room of his local hospital. Or, it is three o'clock in the morning and a child develops an earache; her mother takes her to the ER. In both instances, these people may have health insurance and use the ER only because, at the moment, they have nowhere else to go.

However, a main reason for overcrowding is the number of visits by people with low incomes and little or no insurance. They tend to use the ER as a primary-care doctor's office, for instance, to treat a high fever or an injury that is infected.

Specialties

Some nonprofit hospitals are specialized or have specialty centers, such as St. Jude's facility for children in Memphis, Tennessee, or the Center for Cardiovascular Disease in Women at Brigham and Women's Hospital in Boston, Massachusetts, an affiliate of Harvard Medical School. The latter is dedicated to making women aware of heart disease and related complications.

Hospitals primarily exist for inpatient care. However, they do give outpatient care in emergency rooms and specialty clinics, such as a surgicenter. In this kind of facility, a patient is admitted early

St. Jude, Specializing in Children

A well-known example of a specialized institution is St. Jude Children's Research Hospital in Memphis, Tennessee. It was founded in 1962 by actor-comedian Danny Thomas and named for the Catholic patron saint of hospitals, Saint Jude Thaddeus. St. Jude treats children with cancer and other catastrophic illnesses regardless of the family's ability to pay. Thomas also founded the American Lebanese Syrian Associated Charities (ALSAC), which is the fund-raiser for St. Jude. Patients come from all over the United States and many foreign countries to receive treatment at St. Jude. Depending on the illness and severity, there may be a waiting list for admission.

Work at St. Jude has helped to dramatically increase the survival rates of children from devastating illnesses. For example, its doctors have helped to improve the survival rate for acute lymphoblastic leukemia (ALL). This disease of the white blood cells is the most common cancer in children, accounting for 23 percent of cancers in those younger than age fifteen. When St. Jude opened, the survival rate for children with ALL was less than 5 percent; today, some 85 percent survive five or more years. In 1996, Dr. Peter Doherty of St. Jude was named co-winner of the Nobel Prize in Physiology or Medicine for his work related to the immune system.

in the morning and is sedated for the surgery, which is usually elective. An elective surgery is one that need not be performed on an emergency basis because delaying it will not generally cause an unfavorable outcome. For example, cosmetic surgery, such as liposuction or rhinoplasty, is usually elective. After surgery, the patient is observed during the day until the anesthetic wears off, and he or she goes home later in the day with a friend or relative. The Oral & Maxillofacial Surgery and Pharmacology Clinic at Baylor University in Dallas, Texas, is an example. In most cases, costs are reduced because no overnight stay is involved. Those with serious surgeries or whose medical health is questionable are not admitted. If complications occur after surgery in the Baylor clinic, the patient may be admitted to the Baylor University Medical Campus.

Instead of going to a hospital emergency room for quick medical attention, a patient may go to an urgent-care center. First in existence in the 1970s, about 17,000 of them are now located around the country. These profit-oriented centers provide unscheduled, walk-in care. Patients generally need immediate attention for problems not serious enough to warrant a trip to the emergency room, such as a sprained ankle. They also may offer free blood-pressure checks to anyone or blood-sugar checks for diabetics on certain days. They generally accept all insurance plans except Medicaid. Those without insurance are charged a flat fee, usually ranging from about $90 to $150. The urgent-care center is not generally open 24/7; some may operate nine-to-five or on another fixed schedule.

Nursing Homes, Hospice, and Long-term Care

People who need constant attention and help with everyday living chores may be cared for in nursing homes, skilled nursing facilities, or skilled nursing units. The patients include the elderly and younger adults with physical problems. Some people may spend their last years in a nursing home; others may be there for a short time to recover from a broken hip, for example. Medicare covers nursing-home stays for a very limited time and for limited purposes.

U.S. nursing homes must always have a licensed nurse on duty. During at least one shift each day, the licensed nurse must be a registered nurse (RN). There are three types of registered nurses. The BSL (bachelor of science) nurse usually completes a four- to five-year program in a college or university. The associate degree nurse means that he or she has completed a two-year program, usually in a community college. The diploma nurse (more common before the 1970s) has usually completed a three-year program in a hospital. In addition, the staff includes LPNs, licensed practical nurses who must be at least eighteen years old and a high school graduate or the equivalent.

Hospice care is also known as end-of-life care. It is paid for by Medicare for those people judged to have six months or less to live and for those who have refused medical intervention. The care is given by health professionals (doctors and RNs) and the many, many volunteers who are vital to the program. Care can take place in the patient's home, a hospice center, a hospital, or a skilled nursing facility. Wherever the patient is, health professionals visit on a regular basis to check on medicines or dress wounds. Home visits might be scheduled for twice a week, for example. The professionals speak with the families, advising them of the patient's condition. Volunteers keep the hospice running. They answer phones, keep medical records, sit and talk with patients when needed, and help to ease what is usually a painful time for both patient and family.

Hospice services vary by state. Florida, for instance, has a comprehensive system. As an example, a patient who is being cared for at home can enter a hospice facility for just a few days if the home caregiver has to be absent or just needs a rest. Some states have too few hospice facilities to offer such an option. The aim of hospice care everywhere is to control pain and other distressing symptoms and to help people who are dying to do so in peace and with dignity.

Long-term care is for people who have a disability or chronic illness. It can be provided at home, in nursing homes, or at facilities within the community. It usually involves assisting people with daily living tasks such as dressing and bathing.

Each year millions of older Americans require long-term care of some kind. But people may need long-term care at any age; for instance, they may suffer a brain injury or other devastating accident that keeps them disabled for months or years.

Generally, Medicare pays for necessary skilled-nursing facilities or home health care. The person must be homebound to receive home health care and when that circumstance changes, the care is quickly terminated. Medicare does not pay for long-term care that is called custodial care, meaning help with daily activities, such as housekeeping.

Minors in the Health Care System

The number of uninsured people in the United States includes millions of children. According to the *New York Times Almanac* (2008), nearly 5 million minors were uninsured in 2006. Generally, they live in homes where the parents cannot afford health insurance or can't get it.

Through the years, the U.S. government has tried in various ways—and with varying degrees of success—to meet the health needs of children. In 1935, for instance, the Aid to Families with Dependent Children (AFDC) was created to give cash to needy families. At first, states gave cash payments to homes with only one parent. Later, two-parent homes were included if just one parent was working and the income was low. It was replaced in 1996 under the Clinton administration by a cash welfare block grant called the Temporary Assistance for Needy Families (TANF). These funds are used to get people off welfare and into jobs that can provide health coverage. President George W. Bush reauthorized it in 2005.

In 1997, during the Clinton administration, the State Children's Health Insurance Program (SCHIP) was created. It was the largest expansion of health-care coverage for children since Medicaid. This federal government program gives money to the states to cover families that cannot qualify for Medicaid funds. The states have some flexibility in how the program is run. The money may be used to expand Medicaid or it may be a separate program. Those with separate programs have more flexibility than those that share Medicaid. They also may use different names such as CubCare in Maine or Dr. Dynasaur in Vermont.

Over the first two years, some one million children were enrolled in SCHIP. However, in 2007, Congress twice tried to authorize expanding the SCHIP budget. Both attempts were vetoed by President Bush. He said that parents with more money might drop their own insurance for the better government option, thereby shifting the focus away from poor children. During his campaign, President Obama vowed to revive the program.

Through government contracts and private grants and endowments, all fifty states and numerous cities have varying degrees of health protection for children. Louisiana, for example, established the Louisiana Children's Code in 1992. It is aimed at protecting children whose physical or mental health needs are at risk, including victims of neglect. The code asserts the right to interfere in a family for the general welfare of the child. The city of Seattle, Washington, established the Center for Children with Special Needs in 1998. It focuses on children with chronic conditions such as asthma, autism, or cerebral palsy. It does not provide medical care but directs families to health professionals.

In all states, family planning and prenatal clinics offer services regardless of age or ability to pay. A family planning clinic usually provides birth control information, yearly medical exams, pregnancy counseling and tests, information on adoption and abortion, and screening for sexually transmitted diseases, including HIV tests.

An example is the Family Planning Associates Medical Group (FPA) of California. It was founded soon after abortion became legal in the state in 1970. The Supreme Court decision in *Roe* v. *Wade* (1973) legalized abortion in all states. Abortions done by the FPA and other medical services were performed at Avalon Memorial Hospital in Los Angeles. With *Roe* v. *Wade*, it became legal to perform abortions outside the hospital. That made it possible for pregnancy and family planning services to be offered to outpatients. FPA set up the state's first large outpatient pregnancy program in Santa Ana. Since then, the services of the FPA have increased, with twenty-four more facilities as far east as Chicago, Illinois. The FPA is now the largest independent family planning service in the United States. Private-practice doctors as well as private and government agencies that do not want to perform abortions refer patients to the FPA. Listed in its services are tests for pregnancy, abortions, birth control information, and sterilization procedures. The doctors who provide these services practice only for the FPA.

Many cities and states run teen clinics with services aimed at low-income, sexually active teenagers. All the services are confidential; the teens are not required to get parental permission for birth control or pregnancy tests. However, most of these clinics encourage teens to talk with the parents or trusted adults about any related problems. An example is Chicago's public health clinic, which opened a special program for teens in 1982. The idea grew out of the observations of the staff at the main clinic. They decided there was a need for a private place where teens could discuss their sexual or medical problems and get advice and help.

Most teen clinics are walk-ins. The teen just has to show up during the clinic's working hours. Some clinics, however, offer appointment times. No one is turned away because he or she cannot pay. Teen clinics can be found online in all major and most large U.S. cities.

Prenatal clinics offer obstetric care to women regardless of ability to pay. The Pregnancy Center & Clinics of the Low Country (PCCLC) in Jasper County, South Carolina, cares for women who are uninsured or underinsured and for those who don't qualify for Medicaid. Prenatal clinics provide tests for pregnancy and sexually transmitted diseases, clothing and equipment for infants, psychological counseling, adoption information, and prenatal care through the sixteenth week of gestation (normal pregnancy usually lasts forty weeks).

The Baby TALK (Teaching Activities for Learning and Knowledge) program was founded in Decatur, Illinois, in 1986, to develop healthy parent-child relationships during the critical early years. It operates in thirty-one states and in Canada. Low-income parents and parents-to-be get counseling and education at the clinics. The program encourages literacy workshops and provides information about how children develop. It also provides hands-on treatment. Parents are invited to bring their new babies to the public library where they are introduced to the children's book section. The staff periodically make phone calls to find out how the parents are coping with stress. If there is a problem, the staff can refer the parent to an agency that can help. If necessary, the Baby TALK staff make home visits. The whole idea is to give the new parents confidence in their ability to take care of their own children.

Military, Veterans, and Native Peoples

The United States also provides health care to its domestic military personnel, retirees, and dependents under TRICARE and on military facilities and in active war areas such as Iraq. There are three options. With TRICARE Standard, a qualified civilian health-care provider can be used for an annual fee. TRICARE Extra allows the patient to choose a provider from a regional contractor network. TRICARE Prime is a health maintenance organization (HMO) program. Providers usually must be chosen from the program's

Marine Joshua Bell, injured in the Iraq War, walks with prosthetic limbs at Walter Reed Army Medical Center. His medical care and rehabilitation are insured because he is a war veteran.

roster. Retirees and their families pay an annual enrollment fee; those on active duty do not.

U.S. military veterans are covered by the Cabinet-level United States Department of Veterans Affairs (VA). It was established in 1988 to replace the old Veterans Administration. The VA is the government's second largest department, after the Department of Defense. Some 230,000 people work at the hundreds of VA medical centers, offices, and clinics. The Veterans Health Administration is the branch responsible for providing health care to veterans.

If a veteran has a service-connected disability of 50 percent or higher (determined by the rating boards of VA regional offices), he or she receives care and medications at no charge. The veteran may also receive a pension, rated on the severity of the disability. Those with lesser or non-service-connected health problems—needing medication for asthma, for instance—are charged significantly reduced fees for their medications.

Health care for federally recognized American Indian tribes (numbering more than five hundred) and Alaska Natives (including the Aleut) is the responsibility of the Indian Health Service (IHS). Part of the Department of Health and Human Services, it was established in 1955 to replace the Bureau of Indian Affairs. Hospitals and clinics run by the IHS give care to any registered American Indian or Alaska Native tribe members; health-care facilities on reservations serve only their own tribal members.

Special Interest Groups

A special interest group is an organized set of people who aim to influence political policy. They do not seek election to public office. There are many special interest groups in many fields in the United States. For example, Greenpeace is concerned with the environment, and the National Rifle Association focuses on gun laws. One of the most powerful and one of the largest special interest groups in the health-care field is the AARP.

The AARP was founded by Dr. Ethel Percy Andrus in 1958. A former high school principal, she had set up the National Retired Teachers Association (NRTA) in 1947 to get health insurance for retired teachers. A few years later, the group was opened to those over age fifty. Originally the American Association of Retired Persons, the name was changed to simply AARP in 1999. The change indicates that it does not focus solely on the retired. In fact, a person must be over fifty but does not have to be retired to be a member.

The AARP is a nongovernment special interest group with some 35 million members. It addresses issues that are important to older Americans. It claims not to support or give money to candidates of any political party. It does, however, lobby on state and national issues.

Improved Health Care for American Indians

In February 2008, the U.S. Senate approved the Indian Health Care Improvement Act for American Indians. It is aimed at eliminating what some call a health-care crisis for this part of the population. The bill provides about $35 million to be spent over the next ten years on building and improving clinics on reservations. It also calls for recruiting more American Indians into the health-care field. The Senate bill also excluded abortions at most American Indian health clinics.

The AARP also offers its members a number of services and products. It is a secondary health insurer to Medicare. Members pay a monthly premium for a plan that generally picks up the fees that Medicare does not pay. Members also receive discounts on such things as vacation packages or rental cars. Programs of the AARP Foundation help low-income, older workers with such things as preparing their taxes or job training.

AARP is not without its critics. Some claim that sometimes the interests of AARP conflict with the interests of its members. They say that members could get better and cheaper insurance policies on their own. AARP admits that its policies are not always the cheapest but feels that it offers a better deal overall than other policies. For instance, AARP insurance policies typically ask for less health data than do most others. That makes it easier for people who are not in excellent health to get coverage. In turn, that makes the pool of policyholders more risky and raises the premium prices.

It should also be remembered that AARP is an insurance company. It acted as such when it endorsed the Medicare part D law, which is of only marginal help to elder citizens with prescription costs.

Research Funding

Research funding generally refers to any money given for scientific research. The government, corporations, and foundations run what is essentially a competition. Potential research projects are evaluated, and since money is always scarce, only the most promising get funding. The two biggest sources of research funding in the United States are the government, through universities and specialized agencies, and the development departments of corporations. Some research money comes from charitable foundations that may want to develop cures for certain diseases.

The Howard Hughes Medical Institute

An example of a private research facility free of government restraints is the Howard Hughes Medical Institute in Chevy Chase, Maryland. It was founded in 1953 by aviator and engineer Howard Hughes. Today, it is one of the largest private funding organizations for biological and medical research in the United States. Its annual investment in this research amounts to about $450 million. It is the second-best-endowed medical research foundation in the world, following Great Britain's Wellcome Trust. Since Hughes's death in 1976, the institute has focused mainly on genetics (how traits and qualities are passed from parents to children), immunology (the study of disease and how the body responds to it), and molecular biology, which is chiefly concerned with understanding how various systems of a cell interact.

The main agency for biomedical and health-related research in the United States is the National Institutes of Health (NIH). It is responsible for about 28 percent of the annual U.S. biomedical research funding. Part of the Department of Health and Human Services, NIH has two sections. One section deals with funding research that is conducted outside the NIH. The other covers only NIH research, most of which takes place in Bethesda, Maryland.

NIH began back in 1887 as the Laboratory of Hygiene. In 1930, it was reorganized into what was known as the National Institute (singular) of Health. Today, it has twenty-seven separate institutes and centers as well as the office of the director. The institutes operate in various health areas. For instance, the National Institute of Environmental Health Sciences in Research Triangle, North Carolina, sponsors programs for students interested in careers in biomedical and biological sciences. The National Institute of Allergy and Infectious Diseases in Hamilton, Montana, studies all aspects of such infectious diseases as malaria, influenza, and AIDS. Other institutes look into aging, cancer, alcohol abuse, arthritis and skin diseases, eye diseases, and the structure of the human gene.

2 Who Pays for Health Care?

Fact: The United States . . . spends much more per
capita on health care than any other country.
—Kaiser Family Foundation, 2007

THE UNITED STATES HAS THE WORLD'S MOST EXPEN-
sive health-care system by a wide margin. One report from the
Organization for Economic Cooperation and Development
(OECD) gave a figure of $5,711 for U.S. spending on health care
per person (in the 2003 reported year). The next highest spender
was Switzerland, with $3,847. Some might imply that higher
U.S. spending is a good thing. Don't you get what you pay for?
Switzerland spent $1,864 per person less than the United States
in the recorded year. But Switzerland's health-care system, according to the World Health Organization (WHO), is ranked
number twenty in the world; the United States is number thirty-
seven. France is ranked number one by WHO, but the French
spent $2,663 less per person in 2003 than did the United States.
Are Americans really getting what they pay for?

Country	WHO Ranking	% of GNP Spent on Health Care
Canada	30	9.9
France	1	9.8
Great Britain	18	8.0
Germany	25	11.1
Italy	2	8.4
Switzerland	20	11.5
United States	37	15.2

2003 figures, *New York Times Almanac,* 2008.

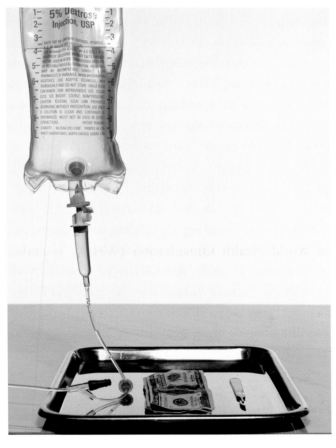

The U.S. health-care system is the most expensive in the world. The recession that started in 2008 brought it dangerously close to needing life support.

Why do Americans spend so much? There seem to be lots of reasons. The costs of new medical technology and prescription drugs are constantly on the rise. The amount of paperwork that keeps the system running is staggering—and costly. The growth of for-profit medical facilities helps to increase costs. More people live to older ages in the United States; that means more people need medical attention at some time. And the uninsured are a big reason for increased costs. When these people need medical help, they usually go to emergency rooms. Or if the uninsured don't seek help at all, they may end up needing intensive or long-term care treatment—again, very expensive.

The gross national product (GNP) is the value of all goods and services produced in a country in one year. Health-care spending is about 15 percent of the GNP in the United States. That compares with about 8 percent in Great Britain, whose health-care system is ranked number eighteen by WHO. According to the National Coalition on Health Care, total spending on U.S. health care "was $2 trillion in 2005. Health care spending is 4.3 times the amount spent on national defense. Health care spending is projected to reach $4 trillion by 2015."

Where does all that health-care money go? Who pays for what?

Most Americans receive medical insurance through their employer. However, that is changing. According to an Economic Policy Institute report, "Fewer employees receive health insurance through their employers than in the past, as coverage has declined from 61.5% in 1989 to 58.9% in 2000 and down to 55.9% in 2004." In addition, the report continues, "those who still receive employer provided coverage are now paying a larger share of those insurance costs." On average, according to a Kaiser Family Foundation release: "Covered workers . . . pay 16 percent of the overall premiums for single coverage and 28 percent for family coverage. . . . Workers in small firms (3 to 199 workers) pay significantly more on average ($4,236 per person annually) compared to larger firms ($2,832 annually)." And when covered workers use the health-care services, they are charged additional payments besides the premium costs. These are usually in the form of copayments, such as a $20 fee (the fee may vary, but $20 to $40 is generally the range) for a visit to an eye doctor.

About 9 percent of Americans with insurance buy it directly from insurance companies. They can't get employer-paid insurance because they are either self-employed, work for a company that doesn't insure its workers, or retired early. In some cases, they may be between jobs and their COBRA (Consolidated Omnibus Budget Reconciliation Act) coverage has run out. Passed in 1986, this legislation gives health coverage to workers and their families for limited periods under certain circumstances; for instance, the job loss was involuntary, or death or divorce forces a change in lifestyle or location. The consumer with private insurance pays premiums; the amount varies widely according to gender, age, and geographic location.

Managed Care

Ever since the system began, employers have been trying to hold down the costs of employee health care. Through the years, the government tried, largely without great success, to regulate health-care costs. But in 1973, the Health Maintenance Organization Act was passed. It gave grants and loans to start or expand a health-maintenance organization (HMO) that would benefit all members, charge the same monthly premium, and be set up as a nonprofit organization. It removed state restrictions if the HMO was certified by the federal government, and it required employers with twenty-five or more workers to offer an HMO option if requested. This last and most important provision, which expired in 1995, let HMOs into a market that had usually been closed to them. So-called managed care began to flourish.

Managed care refers to various ways of financing and delivering health care. Basically, it is a way to contain costs by controlling services. Is this operation really necessary? Is there a more cost-effective way to manage the patient? In traditional medicine, the patient deals directly with the doctor, who decides on a treatment or orders tests generally without first considering how much they will cost. With managed care, the stated aim is the same—appropriate care for the patient—but the delivery is different. The primary-care doctor becomes the manager of a patient's care. In some plans, the patient may have to get a second opinion for a surgery. The patient may be transferred from a hospital to a less expensive facility to recuperate. Expenses become a factor in providing care.

Managed-care organizations in the U.S. health-care system today may differ in details, but they all operate on the same basis of delivering care while controlling costs. The most common of these are health-maintenance organizations (HMOs), preferred-provider organizations (PPOs), exclusive-provider organizations (EPOs), and point-of-service plans (POS).

HMOs started as a response to problems with the fee-for-service model. There was little if any monitoring of the number of medical visits, reasons for tests, costs of drugs, or length of hospital stays. Hospitals actually were paid by the day, and there were incentives for longer stays. Although there have been abuses of the system, today patients are encouraged to take aftercare in nursing homes or at home with aides, which is far less costly.

HMOs deliver health care through contracts with doctors, hospitals, and other medical personnel. The aim is health service at lower costs than traditional care. They try to do that by managing patient care and reducing expenses. The HMO member must usually choose a primary care physician (PCP), who acts as a so-called gatekeeper. He or she sends the patient to a specialist if necessary. In some plans, women can select an obstetrician/gynecologist as well as a PCP. Usually, a visit to an emergency room does not require a PCP's okay. Some HMOs, known as "open access," allow the

Health-maintenance organizations changed the way health care is consumed and delivered in this country—and for every proponent, there is a detractor.

patient to see a specialist without being referred from the PCP. This type of service is more expensive, however.

Kaiser Permanente, based in Oakland, California, is the largest HMO in the United States. It has more than eight million health-plan members in nine states and the District of Columbia and employs 156,000 workers of all types and some 13,000 doctors. It was founded in 1945 by industrialist Henry J. Kaiser and Dr. Sidney R. Garfield. The name comes from Permanente Creek, near Kaiser's first cement plant.

Kaiser Permanente may be the largest HMO, but it was not the first. Dr. Raymond G. Taylor created a temporary health-care system for the Los Angeles Board of Public Works from 1908 to 1912. Baylor University in Texas started a hospital prepayment plan in 1929 to help ease the financial problems of the Great Depression. It was the first of several such plans that eventually joined to form the Blue Cross insurance network.

Kaiser Permanente's history actually began in 1933 when Kaiser and several other construction contractors formed a health-insurance network. Garfield got the contract to care for some five thousand workers. The Permanente Medical Group was reorganized in 1948 and acquired its present name in 1951. Through its growing years, the HMO constantly fought the opposition of the American Medical Association (AMA) as well as various state and local medical societies.

Today, Kaiser Permanente is administered through eight regions: northern and southern California, Colorado, Georgia, Hawaii, the Mid-Atlantic, the Northwest, and Ohio. The Permanente Federation is a separate entity that focuses on making sure patient care and performance are standardized under one policy system. The ultimate governing body is the board of directors.

Those who manage Kaiser Permanente and other HMOs keep their eye on expenses through such methods as a utilization review. How many times did a patient see a doctor last month? How much did the HMO spend on the patient? The aim is to make sure the services are really necessary to give appropriate care. For those with chronic diseases such as diabetes, the HMO may designate a case manager for the patient to make sure the care providers don't overlap.

HMOs generally come in three models. In the staff model, doctors are salaried by the HMO. Their offices are usually in an HMO building, and in some cases they see only HMO patients. In the group model, the HMO has a contract with a physician group practice, which employs the doctors. If the group serves only HMO members, it is called a captive group model. If the group also treats non-HMO members, it is known as an independent group model. Since 1990, the network model is the one most often used by HMOs. In this form, the HMO can have a contract with groups, individual doctors, and independent practice associations.

Throughout their years of operation, HMOs have come under much criticism. They have been the target of many lawsuits. A big complaint is that HMOs are more interested in making money for themselves than in the health of people. Many say that because of HMO restrictions, some patients are not given the necessary care. Sometimes an HMO is held responsible when a doctor it employs performs badly. However, malpractice suits often fail because the HMO does not control the provided health care, but only the way it is financed. Other criticisms include: you can't choose your own doctor (in most cases); the care is impersonal and operates like an assembly line; patients have to give up their private health policies to join an HMO; and there are often long waiting periods for health service delivery.

The PPO (preferred-provider organization) is a group of doctors, hospitals, and other health personnel. They join with an insurer to bring reduced-rate health care to the insurer's clients. The PPO offers much the same services as the HMO, with a couple of significant differences. The monthly fees may be higher because it has greater flexibility. A member may see any doctor he or she chooses or go to any hospital. In an HMO, usually the member is restricted to the organization's list of hospitals. An employee is not always given a choice between an HMO and a PPO. If so, the PPO may be preferred because of its greater flexibility even with the increase in cost. Sometimes, however, the HMO may be the better deal if it offers more providers to the consumer.

Like the HMO, PPOs use a review system to make sure the provided health care is appropriate and within the cost limits. Usually, PPOs have a precertification requirement. For some outpatient surgery and for nonemergency hospital admissions, the insurer must give prior approval.

In the EPO (exclusive provider organization) setup, individual providers or groups of providers offer health care through written agreements with an insurer. The insurer reimburses the client only if the care comes from the designated network of providers. In turn, this network charges lower rates. The EPO and the network set fees for service. The EPO also helps to solve any problems that may occur between the network providers and the clients. EPOs can often offer lower rates than other managed-care facilities. However, they can also have strict limits, and an EPO member cannot go outside the network for care. Even in an emergency, the member may be charged if he or she uses a hospital outside the designated network. (For these reasons, the EPO has the fewest members of the type of health-care providers.) In contrast, the PPO member may be reimbursed for care received outside the designated-provider list.

The POS (point of service) plan has a little of both the HMO and the PPO. The POS is sometimes called an open-ended HMO or an open-ended PPO. As in the HMO and PPO plans, the POS member may choose from a network of doctors and medical facilities. However, the POS member has the option of being treated by doctors outside the network. If the member does so, the claim may not be entirely covered as it would be if the care came from the designated providers. If the POS member works within the network, all the paperwork is done for him or her. If the client goes outside the POS network, he or she has to complete the paperwork. The new POS client chooses a primary-care doctor from a list of preapproved physicians. However, the client does not have to make a choice about seeking treatment inside or outside the network until medical service is needed.

Medicare

In *Powerful Medicines,* Jerry Avorn notes: "The nation resolved the question of whether the government should get involved in medical care decades ago, with the passage of the first Pure Food and Drug Act in 1906 and of Medicare and Medicaid in 1965." Initially, the Pure Food and Drug Act called for government inspection of meat products. It stopped the manufacture and sale of poisonous medicines. The concern was mainly to see that products were correctly labeled. It was legal to buy and sell cocaine-based drugs, for instance, as long as the label was correct. But concerns soon grew about the safety of the products themselves. And that led to a government suit, backed by the Food and Drug Act, against Coca-Cola. The 1909 case was known as *United States* v. *Forty Barrels and Twenty Kegs of Coca-Cola.* The company was charged with putting too much caffeine in the drink, which was thought to be harmful to children. The case dragged on for years with no one proving much of anything. Due to expenses, however, Coca-Cola finally settled out of court in 1917.

But adverse publicity from the case led to two amendments to the Pure Food and Drug Act in 1912. Caffeine was added to the list of habit-forming and deleterious (harmful) substances that had to be shown on labels. The government was now involved in health care.

The Medicare bill that President Lyndon B. Johnson signed in 1965 provides health insurance paid by the U.S. government. After he signed the bill into law, Johnson handed the first Medicare card to former president Harry S. Truman, who was then eighty-one years old. The card, which all Medicare members are issued, contains the member's name and social security number. It signifies that he or she is eligible for the medical benefits prescribed by the law. Members present the card at hospitals or other medical facilities when they apply for treatment.

Medicare covers U.S. citizens or those who have been permanent legal residents for five continuous years and are age sixty-five or over.

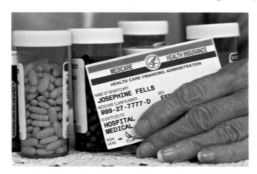

Medicare was passed into law in 1965 to ensure that U.S. citizens would be able to receive medical care regardless of income.

Some people are also covered if they are under sixty-five and have special, often devastating problems, such as disability, permanent kidney failure, or ALS, commonly called Lou Gehrig's disease. Both Medicare and Medicaid are administered by the Centers for Medicare and Medicaid Services in the Department of Health and Human Services. They are financed by payroll taxes, the Federal Insurance Contributions Act, or FICA, and the Self-Employment Contributions Act of 1954.

Medicare originally had two parts: A, which covers hospital insurance, and B, for outpatient insurance. Part C, added later, called medical advantage, allows members with parts A and B to get health services through a Medicare private health plan. Medicare pays the plan a certain amount each month for each member. Members may have to pay a monthly premium besides the Medicare part B premium, and they may pay a fixed amount for each doctor visit. In 2006, part D was added to give seniors more prescription drug coverage. To qualify for Medicare coverage in the hospital or a skilled nursing facility, the patient must stay at least three overnights. Nursing-home stays are covered if they provide skilled care (personal care such as cooking or cleaning is not covered) and if they follow a hospital stay. For instance, if a man breaks his legs and goes to the hospital, then goes to a skilled-care nursing home for rehabilitation, Medicare covers both costs.

A patient can stay in a skilled-nursing home a maximum of one hundred days per ailment. In a hospital, the coverage is sixty days. That includes the room and meals, nursing services, lab tests, X rays, operating-room costs, rehab services such as occupational therapy, intensive care units, use of wheelchairs or other such appliances, and any drugs administered during the stay.

As of 2006, after sixty days in the hospital the patient pays $238 a day from days sixty-one to ninety and the government pays the rest. If the patient is still in the hospital after day ninety, he or she can use a reserve fund. The patient pays $476 a day and the government pays the rest. Sixty days after the patient leaves the hospital or skilled nursing facility, he or she can return to either place and begin a new benefit period. If the patient can't afford the initial charge, Medicaid is called in.

Part B medical insurance helps to pay for some services that part A doesn't cover. It is a voluntary health-insurance plan with monthly premiums. It covers doctor and nursing services, X rays and lab tests, some ambulance transport, chemotherapy, flu vaccinations and blood transfusions, and some outpatient treatments in a doctor's office. Also covered are such equipment as wheelchairs and walkers, oxygen for home use, eyeglasses for cataract surgery, and artificial limbs.

Medicare has many benefits, but it doesn't pay for everything. There are so-called gaps in coverage, such as hospital or skilled-nursing facility costs beyond certain day limits. To cover these gaps, some people opt for a medigap, or supplemental, insurance policy. These are health policies sold by private insurance companies. They help to pay for some of the costs that the original Medicare plan does not cover. There are twelve standard medigap policies, and they must all follow state and federal laws. However, each plan may have different basic and extra benefits and each insurance company decides which medigap policy it will sell. So it is important for the prospective buyer to decide which gaps he or she needs to cover and to compare policies, because the costs of these policies vary. Those interested in a medigap policy can contact their local city or state health facility. In New York State, for instance, medigap buyers can call the New York Health Insurance Assistance Program for help in deciding on the correct policy. It is costly and worthless to pay for a policy that doesn't cover what Medicare doesn't cover.

Medicare also usually doesn't apply outside the United States, meaning members are covered only if they are in the fifty states, the District of Columbia, Puerto Rico, the U.S. Virgin Islands, Guam, American Samoa, and the Northern Mariana Islands. However, there are three exceptions where Medicare will pay outside the United States:

- A person is traveling through Canada from one of the forty-eight states to Alaska. A medical emergency occurs and a Canadian hospital is closer than one in the United States. Medicare will pay only if it determines that the person was traveling to Alaska by the most direct route.
- A medical emergency occurs when the person is in the United States, but a hospital in Canada or Mexico is closer than a U.S. hospital.
- A person lives in the United States, but a foreign hospital is closer to treat a medical condition even if it is not an emergency.

Medicaid

Like Medicare, Medicaid was created in 1965 and is funded by the federal government and the states. It is the country's largest funding source for those with limited income. Unlike Medicare, Medicaid is intended to serve primarily low-income citizens and legal residents, including the disabled and low-income families with children. Although the federal government provides broad program guidelines, each state sets its own rules for eligibility, benefits, and coverage. Each state determines what it considers to be low income. In New York State, for example, a two-person family earning $10,070 or less annually is eligible for Medicaid. A four-person family with children under age nineteen earning $20,500 a year is eligible.

Most but not all states set their income limits based on those of the Supplemental Security Income (SSI) program. Since 1974, this plan, administered by the Social Security Administration, gives monthly payments to aged (sixty-five or older), blind, and disabled persons judged to be in need.

States generally determine Medicaid limits in one of two ways.

Categorically Needy bases eligibility on a person's income and assets (such as a house) alone. Medically Needy bases eligibility on income and assets plus medical costs. A person may have income and assets above the low-income limits but high medical costs that make him or her eligible for Medicaid.

Some people are eligible for both Medicare and Medicaid programs. Medicaid covers a greater range of services, such as paying for most long-term care both at home and in nursing facilities. Medicaid also pays many of the costs that Medicare doesn't cover regarding hospital and doctor bills, such as the 20 percent of approved doctors' fees that Medicare doesn't pay.

Medicaid may go by different names in different states. For instance, it is called eMedNY in New York and MediCal in California. States don't have to participate in the Medicaid program but all have done so since Arizona joined in 1982. Some states use private health-insurance companies as subcontractors; others pay the doctors and hospitals directly.

Although a person must have a limited income determined by each state to get Medicaid, even poverty doesn't mean he or she qualifies. There are many different requirements to be eligible for the service. There are special rules for disabled children at home, for those in nursing homes, for pregnant women with a family income below the poverty level, for those with disabilities, and for the aged with low incomes.

Medicaid is also available for HIV patients. In fact, it is the largest source of medical coverage for people with HIV/AIDS. Despite improvements in treatment, this disease can be disabling, causing many patients to leave or be unable to enter the workforce. According to the Centers for Medicare and Medicaid Services (CMS), Medicaid spent $6.3 billion, or half of federal spending, on HIV/AIDS care in 2006. More than 50 percent of people living with AIDS in the United States use Medicaid to pay for medical services and prescription drugs.

Controlling Asthma Treatment Costs

Asthma is a chronic disease of the airways that causes wheezing and coughing and sometimes severe breathing problems. It affects some nine million children and about twenty million adults in the United States. Many of them rush to the ER for emergency measures when an attack occurs. This kind of emergency room use is costly. Programs aimed at reducing the disease can end up reducing ER costs as well.

Such a program, the Harlem Children's Zone Asthma Initiative, began in 2002. It is based at New York City's Harlem Hospital Center. The program conducted a study of childhood asthma in Harlem, a largely African-American section of the city. The disease is often prevalent in poor areas. The Harlem program tested children in a sixty-block area around the hospital. The discovered rate was five times above the national average. Parents and children were taught to manage their asthma by a combination of medicines and doctor/nurse visits. People were shown how to improve their environment, like getting rid of mold or dust mites or cigarette smoke.

The result was a drop from 35 to 8 percent of children who went to the ER or an unscheduled doctor visit for treatment. Overnight hospital stays for treatment went from 8 percent to none over the same period. Experts say that this kind of program not only can help control the disease, it can cut the costs of treating it as well.

In early 2006, the Deficit Reduction Act became law. It set up a new way to finance Medicaid health services, called the Health Opportunity Account (HOA). The aim is to make Medicaid users more aware of the costs of their own care. "That's especially needed in Medicaid," said Grace-Marie Turner, president of the Galen Institute, a health policy research organization, "because people on Medicaid have had very little exposure to the actual cost of their health care consumption." Those with an HOA who leave Medicaid can use the remaining money in their accounts to pay for health care or they can use it for job training or education. Turner feels that allowing people to use the money for something they really want will be a savings incentive. However, some disagree with Turner's outlook. They fear that these accounts could ask a person with limited income to pay a high deductible at the outset, before he or she could get any benefits. What happens if an HOA user spends all the account money but hasn't yet met the deductible? The law limits the HOA to a trial run of ten states for five years; after that the government may or may not extend the program.

States also get waivers from the federal government for managed-care programs. Medicaid consumers take part in a private health plan that gets state monthly premiums. Most states today cover a large percentage of their Medicaid users with managed-care plans.

Another Medicaid plan, the Health Insurance Premium Payment Program (HIPP), operates in some states. HIPP may pay for private health insurance for a Medicaid user under some circumstances. Suppose a person is on Medicaid or eligible for it and health insurance becomes available through an employer. HIPP will decide if it is cheaper to use the employer's private plan or pay through Medicaid. This plan might be especially helpful to families with access to private insurance but who have children under nineteen who qualify for Medicaid. The entire family in this instance might be covered by HIPP.

Mental Health Care

According to the *Archives of General Psychiatry*, "An estimated 26.2 percent of Americans ages 18 and older—about one in four adults—suffer from a diagnosable mental disorder in a given year." That translates to more than 57 million people.

Mental disorders fall into seven major categories: degrees of depression; bipolar disorder (extreme mood swings, once called manic-depression); suicide; schizophrenia (brain disorder that might include hearing voices or feeling persecuted); anxiety and panic disorders; obsessive-compulsive (OCD) behavior (including distressing thoughts and repetitive actions); and post-traumatic stress disorder (PTSD: severe fear or numbness following a terrifying experience such as rape). Other mental problems include agoraphobia (fear of traveling or leaving the home); eating disorders (from anorexia nervosa where the person has a distorted body image and is afraid to eat, to uncontrollable episodes of overeating called binge eating); ADHD (attention deficit hyperactivity disorder, a common mental disorder in children that affects the ability to function in school or other settings); autism (a brain disorder that impairs social communication and interaction); substance-related disorders (misuse of alcohol or drugs); and Alzheimer's (a form of dementia usually affecting older adults).

An article in *USA Today* reported that only about one-third of Americans suffering from some form of mental illness get treatment. And that treatment, says the *Washington Post*, is likely to come "after a decade of delays. . . . and the treatment they receive is usually inadequate." The most effective health care for most mental illness is with a psychologist or psychiatrist. Psychiatric treatment involves individualized plans that may include talk therapy and medication. That often involves the entire family. Treatment can be lengthy and expensive.

Psychologist
or
Psychiatrist?

A psychologist studies all aspects of behavior and treats patients in hospitals, clinics, schools, and private practice. There are many different types of treatment, including clinical (the most common), which helps people cope with illnesses, injury, or severe crisis, and counseling, which provides help with everyday living. Clinical and counseling psychologists must have a doctoral degree, which requires five to seven years of graduate study. They must also complete a one-year internship.

A psychiatrist is a medical doctor specializing in diagnosis, treatment, and prevention of mental illness. As physicians, they can order a full range of laboratory and psychological tests in the treatment of patients. Their education includes college and medical school. As new doctors, they spend the first year of residency training in a hospital and treating a wide range of mental illnesses. They spend at least three more years in a psychiatric residency where they learn to diagnose and treat these disorders.

Who pays for it? Mental health care is not a separate benefit under Medicare, but patients are covered through services in parts A through D. If a patient needs psychiatric care and goes to a Medicare-participating psychiatric hospital, part A covers 190 days. But that's it. Medicare will not pay any more for psychiatric care during the rest of a patient's lifetime. But if the patient goes to a general hospital and gets a psychiatric diagnosis, there is no 190-day limit.

A primary physician cannot charge a Medicare patient specifically for the diagnosis of depression, although many elderly people are depressed and go to a doctor's office for this problem.

Medicare provides outpatient services for the mentally ill, including diagnostic testing and office visits to monitor how well prescribed drugs are working. There is a 50 percent coinsurance rate for psychotherapy services. Medicare also pays independent mental health providers such as psychologists, social workers, nurse specialists, and nurse practitioners. In January 2006, Medicare began paying for outpatient prescription drugs for mental illnesses under part D.

Medicaid also covers services for the mentally ill. According to the National Alliance on Mental Illness, Medicaid makes up about 50 percent of overall public mental health spending. Mental health benefits are not explicitly named in Medicaid coverage, but they come under home- and community-based services such as transportation assistance. Benefits also include long-term care for the mentally ill, and there is no waiting period for coverage. Anyone who meets the income and disability limits can qualify.

3 **Who Regulates Health Care?**

Fact: Every year, 18,000 Americans die prematurely
because they have no health insurance.
—National Academy of Sciences' Institute of Medicine

THE DEPARTMENT OF HOMELAND SECURITY PROTECTS U.S. territory from terrorist threats and attacks and responds to natural disasters. Another government agency, the Centers for Disease Control and Prevention (CDC), might also be called a department of homeland security. Its mission is to protect U.S. public health and safety.

Centers for Disease Control and Prevention

The CDC is based in Atlanta, Georgia, and is part of the Department of Health and Human Services. It has ten other locations in the United States, including Anchorage, Alaska, and Puerto Rico, as well as staff members in state and local health agencies and in health offices at various ports of entry. The CDC works with state health departments to keep the public informed about health decisions and potential epidemics such as the flu or the spread of diseases such as AIDS. It also notifies the public of workplace dangers such as asbestos contamination. In that case, the CDC would propose guidelines to assess the risk that workers face. The Occupational Safety and Health Administration (OSHA) would actually draft the proposed rule to be enforced. Both of these agencies work to improve U.S. health overall.

In 1946, a World War II agency known as Malaria Control in War Areas became the basis for the CDC. The new agency was called the Communicable Disease Center and was located in Atlanta, Georgia. Malaria was then a problem in many of the southern states. It is still a very common infectious disease worldwide. Malaria is transmitted by the female *Anopheles* mosquito and brings on a severe flu-like illness. At its worst, it can cause coma and death. In 2008, for example, malaria accounted for 2 percent of all deaths worldwide and 9 percent of deaths in Africa. In the first year of operation, CDC workers were mainly engaged in killing mosquitoes, using the insecticide DDT. At the time, the CDC staff was mostly nonmedical personnel; they had to know how to drive trucks or use a shovel in the war against the mosquito.

In 1947, the CDC paid Emory University a token ten dollars for fifteen acres of land, on which its headquarters are located today. (Actually, the land was paid for by Coca-Cola chairman Robert Woodruff, who had an interest in malaria control. He said mosquitoes were a problem when he went hunting.) From that beginning, the organization has become the country's main health promotion and prevention agency. Its staff, which numbered 369 in the first year of operation, now includes nearly 15,000. They are engineers, scientists, economists, veterinarians, nurses, and physicians, to name just a few specialists.

Although it is still known by its original initials of CDC, the name change in 1992 to Centers for Disease Control and Prevention reflects its increased role as the nation's health overseer. Because of its extensive work with communicable diseases, it is recognized as a world authority. It is also one of the few Biosafety Level 4 labs in the United States. Biocontainment refers to safety precautions against biological agents. There are four safety levels, the higher numbers indicating greater risk to the environment.

The World War II agency formed to control the malaria that was bringing down U.S. troops became the basis for a national agency that has been in charge of disease control and research ever since. Here, an entomologist examines a malaria-transmitting mosquito under a microscope.

Biosafety Level 1 includes work with such bacteria and viruses as varicella (chicken pox). The dangers from these materials are low level, requiring personnel to wear only protective gloves and face masks. The lab itself does not need to be separated from the main facility. Decontamination mostly involves washing with an antibacterial soap and keeping lab surfaces clean with disinfectants.

Biosafety Level 2 involves bacteria and viruses that are moderately hazardous to humans, such as hepatitis A, B, and C, mumps, Lyme disease, or influenza. Personnel who work there have specific training in handling these agents. When work is in progress, passage into and out of the laboratory is limited.

Biosafety Level 3 deals with potentially lethal diseases such as anthrax, typhus, Rocky Mountain spotted fever, and yellow fever. Anthrax is an acute disease caused by bacteria that can affect both humans and animals. The name comes from the Greek word for coal and refers to the black skin lesions that develop on the victim. Typhus is an illness caused by bacteria passed to humans through contact with infected insects. The victims develop fever, weakness, and severe muscle aches. Rocky Mountain spotted fever is a severe illness caused by bacteria that spreads to humans through ticks. Without prompt treatment, it can be fatal. Yellow fever is an acute viral disease and the source of horrific epidemics through the years. The name refers to the yellow color of the infected victims. The labs that work with all these diseases have special design features. The personnel who work in them are not only highly trained, but are supervised by scientists with specific knowledge of these agents. When work is in progress, access to the lab is limited.

Biosafety Level 4 involves dangerous agents that can be fatal to humans such as the Ebola virus, smallpox (although there is a vaccine), or various exotic fevers. Only a few labs exist at this level in the United States, including at the CDC. The staff have specific and thorough training in these types of agents. They wear hazmat suits (similar to spacesuits) and have self-contained oxygen supplies. At the lab entrance and exit, there are showers and ultraviolet light rooms to remove all traces of the materials. Doors are electronically secured, and access is strictly controlled by the lab director. These labs are entirely separated from the main facilities or they are in a controlled area that is isolated from all other building sites.

The CDC is also one of only two places in the world designated as the "official" holder of the deadly smallpox virus. Smallpox was a human scourge for centuries. It is highly contagious. The victim comes down with chills, fever, nausea, and muscle aches. Then a rash appears that turns into pus-filled lesions. If the victim survives, the rash scars may be permanent. In the most severe form, the fatality rate is 50 percent among those who are not vaccinated.

The first smallpox epidemic recorded was in 1350 BCE and reached Europe around the fifth century CE. Since that time, millions of people have died of the disease. However, people began to realize that someone who survived smallpox was immune for the rest of his or her life. In the 1790s, English doctor Edward Jenner discovered the vaccination for smallpox. Over the years, the vaccine destroyed the disease so thoroughly that the United States stopped smallpox vaccines in 1972, except for military personnel, who it was thought might be sent to places where there was no vaccine. In 1979, the World Health Organization (WHO) issued a declaration on smallpox. WHO, the United Nations agency created in 1948, is concerned with worldwide public health. It declared that the smallpox virus had been wiped out worldwide. The United States stopped vaccinating military personnel against the virus in 1990. Besides the CDC, the other official holder of the deadly virus is the VECTOR research center in Russia.

Food and Drug Administration

In addition to such government facilities as the CDC keeping watch on public health, there are regulatory bodies that do the same. One is the Food and Drug Administration (FDA), an agency of the Department of Health and Human Services. The FDA regulates food types, drugs, vaccines, dietary supplements, cosmetics, veterinary products, medical devices, and more. It also enforces section 361 of the Public Health Service Act. That deals with the spread of communicable diseases between states or between foreign countries and the United States.

CDC's
Russian
Counterpart

Along with the CDC, the State Research Center of Virology and Biotechnology, known as VECTOR, is the official repository of the smallpox virus. It is a highly sophisticated biological research facility located in Koltsovo, Novosibirsk Oblast, a secluded area in Russia. An entire elite army regiment guards the center. So do motion sensors, fences, and cameras. Like the CDC, VECTOR has a Level 4 lab for work with infectious and life-threatening diseases.

The Food and Drug Act was signed by President Theodore Roosevelt in June 1906. Until that time, some federal and state laws tried to protect the public against mislabeling of food products and other schemes. Among other things, the new act penalized the transportation of so-called adulterated food. That meant food that was colored to conceal damage or had fillers added to change the quality or strength. It also banned food and drug misbranding. The responsibility for carrying out these regulations went to the Bureau of Chemistry, headed by Harvey Washington Wiley. In 1927, the bureau became the Food, Drug, and Insecticide organization. In 1930, it became the Food and Drug Administration, or FDA.

Early in the 1930s, it became clear that FDA laws were inadequate. But it took the Elixir Sulfanilamide tragedy to push Congress into action. More than one hundred people in fifteen states died and many more became ill during September and October 1937. They had taken sulfanilamide, a drug that in tablet or powder form was effective in curing throat infections. But Harold Watkins, chief chemist at S.E. Massengill Company in Bristol, Tennessee, discovered that sulfanilamide could be dissolved in diethylene glycol. The result was a mixture that tasted and smelled better than the original. Soon shipments of Elixir Sulfanilamide were sent all over the country.

At the time, there were no laws that tested new drugs to see if they were toxic. So, no one tested Massengill's new concoction. But diethylene glycol was normally used as an antifreeze and is a poison. The first shipments went out in September and the first deaths were reported in early October. Although many people died, the death toll would have been far higher were it not for the efforts of federal and state health agencies to track down the prescriptions. Watkins committed suicide while awaiting trial.

Out of that deadly experience came the Federal Food, Drug, and Cosmetic Act, signed by President Franklin Roosevelt in June 1938. It is the basis for FDA authority today. It forces a review of new drugs before they hit the market. It bans false claims for drugs. It mandates factory inspections where the drugs are made. It set higher standards for food control, and it also covered cosmetic and therapeutic devices. And, according to *FDA Consumer* magazine: "25 years later, it saved the Nation from an even greater drug tragedy—a thalidomide disaster—like that in Germany and England."

In 1959, Tennessee senator Estes Kefauver headed a committee looking into pharmaceutical drug companies. It was learned that some of the companies gave experimental drug samples to doctors. The doctors then gave the untested drugs to patients and were paid for collecting the data on their reactions. Kefauver and the committee called for amendments to the Food, Drug, and Cosmetic Act. They were aided by the thalidomide disaster in 1961, mainly in England and Germany but also to some degree in Canada and the United States. Pregnant women were given the sedative thalidomide to calm anxious nerves. The result was thousands of birth defects. Generally, the newborns were missing limbs or parts of limbs. The shocking pictures helped to pass the 1962 Kefauver-Harris amendment, also called the Drug Efficacy Amendment. Among other things, the law required informed consent of the consumer when testing experimental drugs. Before the amendment, drug companies only had to show that their new products were safe. Now they had to show that the new drug was both safe and effective. However, many herbals and so-called natural medicines—those with no artificial ingredients—are exempt from FDA requirements.

The FDA has many branches that help do its work. The Center for Food Safety and Applied Nutrition (CFSAN) is responsible for the safety and labeling of most food and cosmetic products. The Center for Drug Evaluation and Research sets requirements for new prescription drugs, generic drugs, and over-the-counter (nonprescription) drugs. The Center for Biologics Evaluation and Research (CBER) watches over blood, blood products, vaccines,

Thalidomide—
Then and Now

The thalidomide disaster might have been far worse in the United States were it not for the stubbornness of an FDA medical officer. Frances Oldham Kelsey's first assignment when she joined the FDA in 1960 was to examine the data on thalidomide. She found the application data weak and inadequate. Kelsey insisted that the drug company, Richardson-Merrell, conduct further tests.

According to FDA historian John P. Swann, the tug-of-war between the drug company and Kelsey was fierce. "It's fascinating to see how many letters and communications went back and forth. She was asking for additional data, and what they were sending was in her eyes insufficient to answer the questions she was raising. She was increasingly pressured by the sponsor to get the drug approved. She didn't back down."

Because of her insistence, the drug company withdrew its application in March 1962, thus possibly saving many more infants from birth defects. For her work, President John F. Kennedy gave Kelsey the President's Award for Distinguished Federal Civilian Service.

After thalidomide was banned, researchers continued to conduct experiments with the drug. It is now in use under certain tightly controlled conditions. In 1998, the FDA approved it for treatment of a certain type of lesion under the brand name Thalomid. In 2006, the drug received FDA approval in some circumstances for patients with multiple myeloma, cancer of the body's plasma cells. According to the Patient Information Sheet (October 2006) of the FDA Center for Drug Evaluation and Research, if there is no other treatment available, a woman of childbearing age may be given Thalomid if she agrees to it in writing.

The U.S. Food and Drug Administration was formed to prevent dangerous food and drugs from reaching consumers. The thalidomide debacle—which caused babies whose mothers had taken the medication during pregnancy to be born with withered limbs—would've been much worse if not for the persistence of an FDA medical officer.

and the like. The Center for Devices and Radiological Health (CDRH) approves all medical devices. The Center for Veterinary Medicine (CVM) regulates food and drugs for animals, but not vaccines, which come under the U.S. Department of Agriculture. The other branches include the National Center for Toxicological Research, the Office of Regulatory Affairs, and the Office of the Commissioner.

The FDA is the watchdog over many, many products that affect the health of Americans. Its authority is widespread, so much so that government and nongovernment organizations keep an eye on the watchdog. Even so, the FDA gets its share of complaints and criticism. For instance, there were many complaints over the heparin mistake, reported by the *Washington Post* in early 2008. Its February 19 headline read: "FDA Says It Approved The Wrong Drug Plant." The confusion concerned the blood thinner heparin. Millions of people each year take the drug to prevent complications after surgery, among other uses. But by the end of 2007, there were hundreds of reports of bad reactions from heparin, such as breathing difficulties. Four people died. The FDA admitted its mistake. When the Chinese company that makes an ingredient for heparin applied for approval, the FDA thought it had already inspected the firm because it had inspected another factory with a similar name. It immediately sent a team of inspectors to China. Some in Congress believe that the FDA is not large enough to inspect the thousands of drugs and ingredients that are imported.

What kind of safety net *does* the FDA have for testing drugs? The three-phase process—although not without error, as seen in the heparin scandal—aims to be thorough and painstaking. But as the FDA itself admits, no drug is absolutely safe. An adverse reaction is always a slight possibility.

Before phase 1 begins with a new drug, animal tests are performed. If the review board approves the results, the drug is now ready for clinical testing. This is the first time that the drug will be used on humans. The subjects are sometimes patients, but are more likely to be healthy volunteers, as many as eighty in a testing. The study aims to answer these questions: How effective is the drug? Does it do what it's supposed to do? What are possible side effects?

If all of that goes well, it's on to phase 2. These tests are more detailed and involve more subjects. Can a patient with a specific condition be treated efficiently with this drug? Phase 3 may involve a few thousand people. The effects of the drug are studied in even greater detail.

This whole process can take a long time. The FDA says that all the testing of a new drug might go on as long as eight years. To someone with a cancer diagnosis, the disease could cause death well before then. The flip side is that some drugs are safe in the short term but can have harmful effects over time.

For a patient with a life-threatening disease, a drug not yet approved may be allowed under what is known as compassionate drug use. This refers to a terminally ill patient who is given an unapproved drug because none other is available. The FDA calls them investigational drugs, first approved in 1987 for the critically ill.

Compassionate drug use is under tight control. Patients who are not in clinical drug trials may get an unapproved drug either by the expanded access program (EAP) or by single access. A drug company may offer a drug that is not yet approved, for example, in phase 3, to those not in a clinical trial. The FDA might approve the use of the drug if the tests so far have been encouraging; for example, the drug slows the growth of a certain type of tumor. For a patient not in a clinical trial or an EAP, his or her doctor may request its use from the company that is sponsoring the drug. If the company consents, both the drug company and the doctor work together to request permission for use from the FDA.

Another Health Watchdog

A major group that keeps tabs on U.S. health care is the Joint Commission on Accreditation of Hospital Organizations (JCAHO). It is a private, nonprofit organization that was created in 1951. Its name was changed to JCAHO in the 1980s. JCAHO gets millions of dollars each year, mostly from the fees that it charges hospitals for letting them know whether or not they are complying with federal rules. An international branch, the Joint Commission

When Time Matters

Genentech, a drug company in San Francisco, makes a drug called Avastin. It has been approved for the treatment of colon cancer and some lung cancers. But in February 2008, the FDA approved its use with chemotherapy for breast cancer patients. A study showed that the drug caused a reduction of more than 50 percent in the spread of the disease. This shortened time for FDA approval was allowed under the accelerated approval program. The accelerated program allows the FDA to sanction a drug for life-threatening diseases based not on final approval, but on positive clinical test results. According to the FDA, "approval of a drug based on such endpoints is given on the condition that post marketing clinical trials verify the anticipated clinical benefit."

International (JCI), was created in 1997. It surveys hospitals outside the United States.

The JCAHO checks and officially recognizes (meaning it grants the legal credentials to) about 20,000 health-care organizations, including general, children's, and rehabilitation hospitals, home health services, health-care networks, long-term-care facilities, clinical laboratories, and ambulatory-care providers. It looks at a facility's performance in key areas, including whether or not patients receive the promised treatment and services. The JCAHO employs about 650 doctors, nurses, and other health-care professionals to conduct the accreditation surveys. The surveyors do not assess the work of individual doctors.

After the JCAHO surveys a hospital, it lets the hospital know its decision, but it does not open its findings to the general public. Even so, the surveyed hospitals all want to do well. If they are accredited, they are eligible for Medicare and Medicaid funds—a big incentive.

The JCAHO is nearly a monopoly. However, it is not recognized in Pennsylvania and Wisconsin, which have their own such services. Oklahoma does not use it except for outpatient mental health services. In California, it operates jointly with state authorities.

4 The Big Problems: Inefficiency and Inequity

FACT: The leading cause of personal bankruptcy
in the United States is unpaid medical bills.
—Sered and Fernandopulle, *Uninsured in America*

THROUGH THE YEARS, GOVERNMENT LEADERS HAVE
attempted to improve the U.S. health-care system. For instance,
in 1964 President Lyndon Johnson's goals for his Great Society
included health legislation. Medicare and Medicaid were enacted in
1965. However, the United States under President Johnson became
increasingly involved in the war in Vietnam. Health-care reform
faded into the background.

In 1974 President Richard Nixon introduced the Comprehensive Health Insurance Act. It said that employers must buy health
insurance for employees. It set up a federal health plan with payments based on income. Then, a break-in at Democratic National
Committee headquarters at the Watergate complex in Washington,
D.C., ultimately led to the Watergate scandal. President Nixon was
forced to resign in August 1974. His proposed health-care plan
drifted into oblivion.

Under the Clinton administration in 1993, a health-care-reform
package was created by then–first lady Hillary Rodham Clinton. It
said that all citizens had to be enrolled in a qualified health plan.

During the Clinton administration, Hillary Rodham Clinton was at the center of a failed attempt to reform medical insurance. The Obama administration is trying to ensure health care for all.

Coverage and out-of-pocket expenses were detailed. Those below a certain income level paid nothing. Republicans and the insurance industry were major critics. They said the plan restricted a patient's choice and that it was overly bureaucratic—meaning government was too much involved. The Health Insurance Association of America sponsored so-called Harry and Louise commercials, which were very effective. They showed a middle-class couple in despair over the complexity of the proposal. Democrats did not aid the Clinton effort either. Instead of uniting behind the president, many offered plans of their own. Democratic Senate Majority Leader George J. Mitchell introduced a compromise. Among other things, it made small businesses exempt from the proposal. No compromise among the various factions could be reached, and the Clinton health-reform plan was withdrawn in August 1994.

Health Insurance

To talk about health-care reform is to talk about money. It's a fact that health care costs money and it's a fact that health-care costs are always on the rise. How is all this care to be paid for?

Any health plan centers around health insurance. Before the first medical insurance, patients had to pay all costs themselves. In 1911, the first employer-sponsored group disability policy was issued by the Equitable Life Assurance Society of New York. This group policy for Pantasote Leather Company of Passaic, New Jersey, granted insurance coverage to its 121 employees. Later in the century, such policies grew into modern health-insurance programs. They generally cover routine and emergency procedures.

In the 1920s, some hospitals began to offer treatment on a prepaid basis. Baylor College of Medicine in Waco, Texas, set up a health plan for teachers in 1929. For six dollars a year, teachers were guaranteed twenty-one days of hospital (inpatient) care.

Soon, similar plans emerged. The Hospital Service Association (now Blue Cross Blue Shield of Minnesota) first used a blue Greek cross as a symbol for the organization in 1934. The idea spread. The American Hospital Association in Chicago began to use the symbol of the Blue Cross in 1939. It was meant to signify that any organization using the blue cross would maintain high medical standards. The Blue Cross Association was founded in 1960.

The first Blue Shield plan was founded in Tacoma, Washington, in 1917. Monthly fees were paid to bureaus made up of doctors who provided medical care. The first official Blue Shield plan was offered in California in 1939. Today, Blue Cross and/or Blue Shield offer health insurance plans in all fifty U.S. states. In most states, they also administer Medicare.

A health-insurance policy is a contract between an insurance company and the person who buys it. The contract details the kind of care given and what it costs. It can be renewed on a yearly or monthly basis. Several buyer obligations are specified. The premium is the amount the buyer pays each month for the service. The copayment is the amount that the buyer must pay for a doctor's visit before the health plan kicks in. For example, the buyer might be charged a copayment of thirty-five dollars each time he or she visits the doctor. The deductible is the amount the buyer pays before the health plan begins to pay. The deductible might be five hundred dollars a year. Only after that amount is reached will the plan start to pay for medical services. Other obligations may include dollar limits on coverage or certain services that are excluded from the plan. With prescription drug plans, the buyer has to make a copayment and the insurance company picks up the rest of the drug expenses.

Inefficient and Unfair?

Health care in the United States is often inefficient. It is certainly inefficient in its handling of the uninsured, a part of the population that places a great burden on the system. The system itself, which includes perhaps thousands of insurance companies, involves a vast number of people. It is bogged down in heavy administrative costs. These are expenses for things other than providing health-care services, such as employee salaries, paper supplies, and office machinery. A study by Harvard Medical School reported that administrative costs for health care in the United States are nearly double the overhead in Canada. However, the overhead for private insurance in Canada is four times the cost of overhead for the U.S. Medicare program—20 percent versus 5 percent.

In addition, U.S. health care is the most heavily regulated industry in the country. Most of the cost comes from FDA regulations and medical malpractice. A charge of medical malpractice

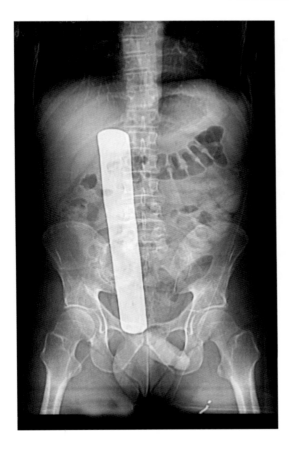

The cost of medical malpractice suits has become a growing issue as the amount doctors have to pay to insure themselves against it has risen. Here, an X ray shows the 13-inch-long, 2-inch-wide surgical retractor accidentally left in the body of a patient after the surgeon removed a tumor. The patient was awarded a $97,000 settlement by the hospital.

claims that the health-care provider (called the defendant) was negligent in his or her treatment of a patient (called the plaintiff). The defendant is usually the doctor, but he or she may be a therapist, nurse, or dentist. The plaintiff may be deceased, in which case the suit is brought on his or her behalf by the administrator of the estate. To win a malpractice case, the plaintiff must show that: (1) the defendant had a duty to perform, as is the case whenever a provider agrees to care for a patient, (2) the provider did not perform the standard of care, as judged by the testimony of experts or by an obvious error, (3) the provider caused an injury, and (4) there are damages to the patient—financial or emotional. Without damages, there can be no claim.

Most Americans with adequate insurance can receive the best health care in the world. Most have access to hospitals with up-to-date facilities and equipment. Most are in the reach of skilled professionals. Most can get care without delay. But not all. U.S. health care is unfairly distributed. Those without adequate insurance or those who live in rural areas may not get to see qualified personnel. The system of government and private programs means that millions of Americans lack coverage. The uninsured may get treatment in the emergency room, but unless they are put into a hospital, they may receive little or no follow-up care.

Even among those who are insured, there are coverage gaps. A person may change jobs and the medical insurance doesn't kick in immediately. Or someone may retire early and not yet be eligible for Medicare. That may mean missing a doctor's visit or not taking medication because it's too expensive. And that results in a decrease in the nation's overall medical health and a greater drain on the system through ER visits and long-term care.

There are also inequities in health care among minorities in America. Many reports indicate that minorities get lower quality care than do white Americans. A study by the Institute of Medicine, an independent research organization, said that even when racial and ethnic minorities have the same income and insurance, they often receive lower-quality health care. They are often less likely to be given appropriate heart medicines or undergo bypass surgery. They are less likely to be placed on the organ transplant list or receive kidney dialysis. They are more likely to get less-desirable procedures, such as a leg amputation for diabetes. Sometimes white doctors stereotype racial and minority patients, regarding them, for instance, as prone to drug abuse. Sometimes white doctors just have difficulty relating to racial and minority patients and, therefore, have difficulty explaining medical procedures or problems.

Much of the problem of lower quality health care is simply that this group in general has less access to good care. African Americans,

Hispanics, American Indians, and Asian Americans reportedly are more likely to be treated by a doctor with less training than the average doctor. Doctors also often don't have a clear understanding of their patients' language or culture.

Racism affects health care. The stress of discrimination can directly affect a person's health; so can living in poor or unhealthy neighborhoods. People who live in poor neighborhoods may not have ready access to a pharmacy for medicines. They are less likely to go to a doctor; even if they have insurance they might not have money for medicines. They are more likely to go to work even when they are feeling ill; they may fear losing their jobs. People who live in a deteriorating neighborhood, with boarded-up or abandoned buildings that collect dust and junk, are more likely to suffer from asthma and other respiratory illnesses.

The Uninsured

About 15 percent of the American population have no health insurance. And according to some studies, that is why a number of Americans die too young. A National Academy of Science study in 2002 said that thousands of Americans die each year because they have no health insurance. The Urban Institute, a nonpartisan association for economic and social policy research, reported the deaths of 22,000 U.S. adults in 2006 because they did not have health insurance. In April 2008, Families USA, a national organization for health-care consumers, claimed that eight people a day die in California for lack of health coverage. These premature deaths are attributed to few medical checkups and screenings and little or no preventive care.

Who are these people at risk and why aren't they covered? The uninsured in America are usually counted in the following categories: by income, age, parents, race, work and citizen status, and company size.

Most of the uninsured in America are the working poor. They

Strange Bedfellows?

A report from Dr. Claudia Henschke of Weill Cornell Medical College in New York City surprised the medical community. Her 2006 study concluded that the widespread use of CT scans could prevent as much as 80 percent of lung cancer deaths. (CT, or computed tomography, scans are X rays enhanced by a computer that produces two-dimensional cross sections of the body's internal organs.) An article in the *New York Times* in March 2008 cast a suspicion of bias on Henschke's study. It said that although the study claimed its funds came from a charity called the Foundation for Lung Cancer: Early Detection, Prevention & Treatment, "small print at the end of the study . . . noted it had been financed in part" by Liggett, maker of several cigarette brands. Dr. Otis Brawley of the American Cancer Society called the Liggett funding "blood money."

It is rare for research studies to accept funds from cigarette makers for fear of undue influence. Although the results of the study seem remarkable, critics caution that more studies are needed to make sure the findings are correct. In addition, the cost of wide use of CTs to look for lung cancer would be extremely high and might be more effectively used in stop-smoking campaigns.

may be earning just enough to scrape by. If they are offered health insurance on the job, they may not be able to afford it. If they work part-time, their employer probably does not offer insurance. But according to the U.S. Census Bureau, in 2005 "one in three Americans without health insurance lived in a household with income greater than $50,000." How can that be? Most of these people actually have low individual incomes but share a household so that the total income allows them to live modestly in many areas of the country. Others are without insurance for a short time, or, conversely, have been earning a high income for just a short time.

The age category of the uninsured usually involves young people. According to a recent report on the CBS *Early Show*, about 15 million Americans between the ages of eighteen and thirty-four "are now living without medical coverage." Some were no longer covered on their parents' plan when they graduated from college. Financial guru Ray Martin offered these two reasons for the lack of insurance for this group: (1) Fewer jobs now have full benefits. Many consulting or freelance positions don't offer health benefits. (2) Young workers often feel they don't want to pay as much as two thousand dollars a year for benefits they don't yet need. Young and healthy for the most part, they can't yet imagine being sick.

Most of the uninsured are without children. A low-income couple may have less incentive to get health insurance if they do not have to care for a child. About half the uninsured are white. About 30 percent of Hispanics are uninsured. Researchers say many Hispanics work in construction or agriculture, jobs that often do not offer health insurance. Most of the uninsured do work. However, they may have jobs that do not offer health care or they do not take it when offered; most cite the high cost of insurance as the reason. They may also be part-time workers, where health insurance is not often an option.

Citizens comprise about 79 percent of the uninsured population. Noncitizens fall into these categories: Hispanic, low income,

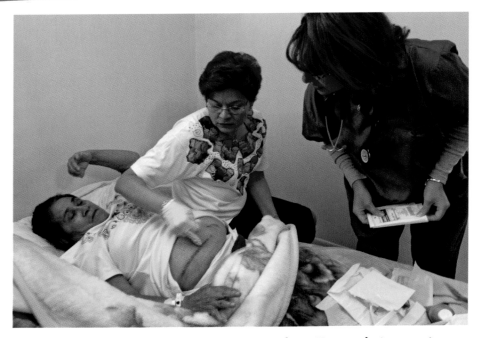

Dr. Soto of the Open Door Clinic pays a visit to Rebecca Munoz, who is recovering from surgery for a hernia that was untreated for years because Munoz lacks health insurance. Even rarer than surgery for the uninsured is follow-up care.

young adults, and those who work for firms of fewer than one hundred employees, where health insurance is often not available.

The insured in the United States have increasingly become a focus of concern. After World War II and the rapid growth of the economy, most Americans had health insurance. Blue-collar workers had union contracts that guaranteed health benefits. White-collar workers were covered by their employers, with whom they generally stayed for long periods. People tended to join a company and stay there, perhaps for their entire working lives. But that is less and less true today. In general, workers no longer spend a lifetime, or even many years, with the same company. In today's frequently changing market, workers average two to three years on the same job. According to a CNET News report, those in the technology field change jobs about every eighteen months. And with constantly rising health costs, some employers look for ways not to cover workers, especially those who may not stay for more than a few years. As a result, millions of Americans are uninsured. They can't afford to be.

Some workers find themselves in what, in insurance lingo, is known as the death spiral. A company sets up a cheap health plan for employees. Everyone may be healthy when they sign up, but as time goes on, people get sick. The cost to insure the unhealthy rises, as do the premiums. Healthy members may be able to find better plans, which leaves the original plan with sicker people and the premiums go even higher. The sick can't afford the coverage any longer, and eventually the company goes bankrupt.

Being uninsured in America often means doing without medical attention—another drain on the system. If a person with asthma can't pay for an inhaler, an attack may lead to the emergency room. Untreated diabetes may mean kidney failure or amputation. An untreated ear infection can cause hearing loss. Small health problems that go unchecked often result in major complications that are not only dangerous, but expensive.

What can uninsured Americans do when they need medical attention? Besides a trip to the emergency room, they cope in various ways. They may skip doses of their medications to make them last longer. They may know a doctor who gives free samples or even writes a prescription even though they aren't covered. Those living near the borders may go into Mexico or Canada to buy over-the-counter drugs that are prescription-only in the United States. However, the U.S. government has cracked down on this border activity, making these sales much more difficult.

The result is not only a hodgepodge of half treatments, it is incredibly expensive. A study in *Health Affairs* found that "approximately half of people in the U.S. who file for bankruptcy cite medical costs as a significant reason for their financial troubles." And most of those had health insurance when the illness began.

Homeless and Uninsured

According to the National Mental Health Information Center, more than 2 million adult Americans are homeless during the course of any given year. Add to that figure about one million homeless children. It is difficult to get an actual count because many of the homeless do not go to city shelters, for instance, or do not eat at soup kitchens where their numbers might be counted. A large number of New York City's homeless, for example, sleep in abandoned buildings, in the subways, or under bridges.

People are homeless for many reasons, including extreme poverty and a lack of affordable housing. The homeless population tends to suffer from serious health problems such as malnutrition, AIDS, and tuberculosis, as well as mental illness, diabetes, and alcoholism. Very few have health insurance of any sort, and fewer have the money to pay for care. As a result of where and how they live, the homeless generally go without treatment until the problem is so bad that it becomes urgent, which may lead to death or a trip to the emergency room. Everyone pays for the cost of this kind of medical attention.

In some big cities, where the homeless tend to congregate, clinics are set up to provide free health care. Since 1987, Health Care for the Homeless projects have been funded by the U.S. Public Health Service. Beyond giving medical care, the projects work to find permanent jobs and shelter in an effort to get people out of homelessness.

Health Care in U.S. Prisons

The United States houses more people behind bars than any other country in the world. Inmates of U.S. jails and prisons number about 2 million. China, with a far larger population, has about 1.5 million imprisoned. Many U.S. inmates suffer from such ailments as hepatitis, tuberculosis, AIDS, substance abuse, and mental illness.

In the case of *Estelle* v. *Gamble* (1976) before the U.S. Supreme

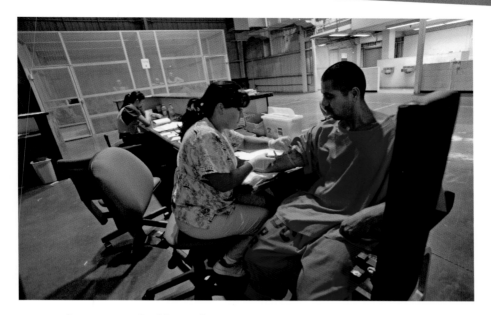

For the most part, health care for prisoners in the United States is free—or the charge is very minimal. The charge to the American public is in the billions.

Court, an inmate of a Texas prison charged the corrections department with cruel and unusual punishment for not treating a back injury he incurred during prison work. Other inmates may have complained in other prisons, but this time the case got to the Supreme Court. Citing the Eighth Amendment, the Court ruled that prisoners have a constitutional right to health care. (Eighth Amendment: Excessive bail shall not be required, nor excessive fines imposed, nor cruel and unusual punishments inflicted.)

On average, each U.S. state spends about 10 percent of its corrections budget on inmate health care. Prison health facilities are accredited by the National Commission on Correctional Health Care. However, it does not monitor health-care abuses in the prisons. Some states require prisoners to make a copayment, ranging from two to ten dollars, for some medical visits. The Department of Corrections in Florida, for instance, charges a three-dollar copayment for nonemergency medical attention. The idea behind the plan is to cut down on unnecessary medical time off by inmates. However, if the prisoner does not have the money for the copay, he or she cannot be refused medical treatment.

Medical Underwriting

Medical underwriting is a process that insurers use to accept or reject those who apply for health or life insurance. The idea is to keep premiums as low as possible. To do so, the insurer asks questions about any preexisting medical conditions. Although this is legal in many states, critics say the practice often means that people with treatable conditions can't get insurance.

In a universal health-care system, with everyone insured, underwriting would be a moot point. But at present, insurers claim that medical underwriting is necessary. Without it, they argue, people would buy health insurance only if they were already sick or pregnant. That would put a further drain on the health-care system. Diseases such as arthritis or heart problems might make someone uninsurable, but so could being twenty-five pounds overweight.

In some states, medical underwriting is illegal. If you can pay for health coverage, you can get it. However, those states also have the highest premiums for personal health insurance.

So long as a person pays the premium on a policy, supposedly it is guaranteed for life regardless of any change in health status. That is not always the case, however. Also, a policy may be cancelled if the insured gave false information on the application.

The Anti-Patient-Dumping Law

In 1986, Congress passed the Emergency Medical Treatment and Active Labor Act (EMTALA). Some call it the anti-patient-dumping law. According to the American Academy of Emergency Medicine, EMTALA "requires hospital emergency departments (EDs) to provide any individual coming to their premises with a medical screening exam (MSE) to determine if an emergency condition or active pregnancy labor is present. If so, the hospital must supply either stabilization prior to transferring the patient or a certification (signed by the physician) that the transfer is appropriate and meets certain conditions."

EMTALA made it illegal for emergency rooms to refuse to treat people because they cannot pay or have insufficient insurance. It also stopped the practice of discharging emergency patients because their treatment would cost too much. Only after the screening exam to determine the illness or injury can a patient be referred to a clinic or primary-care physician.

EMTALA applies to participating hospitals—those that accept payment under the Medicare program. That means most U.S. hospitals, except Shriners Hospitals for Children, Indian Health Services, and military VA hospitals. Even though the law requires hospitals to admit patients for emergency treatment, EMTALA does not pay for this care. It places the financial burden on the hospitals and emergency physicians. Therefore, some argue that the law is straining an already overburdened system. A large percentage of ER treatment is not covered. When medical bills are not paid, the provider may transfer the costs to those who can pay, meaning those who do have insurance are paying for those who do not. Or else, the provider absorbs the loss. Sometimes this results in the closing of ERs, which overcrowds others nearby—another drain on the system.

5 U.S. Health Care and Politics

FACT: Americans pay higher prices for
prescription drugs than anyone else in the world.
—Bartlett and Steele, "The Health of Nations," *The New Yorker*

THE PHARMACEUTICAL INDUSTRY IS VERY BIG BUS-
iness in the United States. Its yearly revenue runs into billions of
dollars. Even with that price tag, pharmaceuticals make up only about
12 percent of total U.S. health-care costs.

Pharmaceutical companies are right in the middle of a major
political issue—the cost of prescription drugs. These costs are on
the rise, meaning that many Americans go without the medicines
they need or they skip doses to save money. Also worrisome is the
rise of prescription drug abuse, especially by teenagers.

The Pharmaceutical Industry

Pharmaceutical, or drug, companies are in the business of
researching, developing, advertising, and selling drugs, mainly for
health care. Most basic research on development is done at the
National Institutes of Health (NIH) or at universities. The "new
drug" advertised by drug companies is often an older medicine in
a different formulation; for instance, it can now be used once a day
instead of two or three times. In this way, the drug companies can
obtain a new patent. Government laws and regulations monitor
a company's every move. These companies are very successful;

Drugs, drugs, and more drugs. Almost all of us take at least some over-the-counter medications, let alone prescription drugs. Among the elderly, a daily dose of ten to fifteen—or even more—prescription drugs is far from unusual.

prescription drug sales in the United States, as reported in *USA Today*, "reached $286.5 billion in 2007." Drug companies are also very influential. Their great influence comes from their products. Selling prescription drugs is not like selling dishwashers or bicycles. People can live without those items, but in many instances they cannot live without the drugs that keep them healthy or free of pain. That fact gives drug industries a lot of power. It also sets them up for a lot of praise—and a whole lot of criticism.

Pharmacists and drugstores have been around for centuries. Major pharmaceutical companies developed in Europe and the United States in the early twentieth century, aided by the discovery of drugs such as penicillin. With their growth came laws concerning testing and labeling.

The real growth of the pharmaceutical companies started in the 1950s. The structure of genetic material was discovered, and the DNA era dawned. In 1950, Mayo Clinic researcher Edward Kendall discovered the drug cortisone to treat arthritis and won the Nobel

79

The Pharmaceutical Top Ten

Ranked by health-care revenue, these are the world's top ten pharmaceutical companies.

Source: Med Ad News, September 2007

	Name	Founded	Headquarters	Employees	Revenue (in millions)
1.	Johnson & Johnson	1887	New Brunswick, NJ	138,000	$53,324
2.	Pfizer	1849	New York, NY	122,200	$48,371
3.	Bayer	1863	Leverkusen, Germany	106,200	$44,200
4.	GlaxoSmithKline (by merger of Burroughs Wellcome & Glaxo Laboratories)	2000	London, England	106,000	$42,813
5.	Novartis (by merger of Sandoz & Ciba-Geigy)	1996	Basel, Switzerland	102,695	$37,020
6.	Sanofi-Aventis	2004	Paris, France	100,735	$35,645
7.	Hoffman–La Roche	1896	Basel, Switzerland	100,289	$33,547
8.	AstraZeneca	1999	London, England	98,000	$26,475
9.	Merck & Co.	1891	Whitehouse Station, NJ	74,372	$22,636
10.	Abbott Laboratories	1888	Abbott Park, IL	66,800	$22,476

Prize for medicine. In 1955, Jonas Salk announced a vaccine to end the dreaded polio epidemics, which crippled so many children and adults for so many years. New instruments and new medical techniques aided in the discovery of new drugs to cure human illnesses.

Drugs became very popular in the 1960s, when major tranquilizers and antianxiety pills came on the scene. These compounds ushered in the so-called drug era. Wallace and Wyeth labs marketed meprobamate, known commercially as Miltown and Equanil. The drug was supposed to make you happier, less depressed, a better worker . . . a better everything. Miltown became so popular as a cure-all that Milton Berle, perhaps the most watched TV comic of the time, called himself Miltown Berle. It was estimated that within a year, about 5 percent of Americans were taking Miltown. In 1966, Mick Jagger of the Rolling Stones even sang about the drug and its calming influence on mothers dealing with their children.

Unfortunately, no one talked about Miltown's side effects. It was later found that the cure-all drug could become addictive and dangerous if taken with other drugs.

But the popularity of these antianxiety drugs was nothing compared to one of the biggest-selling pharmaceutical drugs in history. Marketed by Hoffman–La Roche, it is called Valium. Until the late 1980s when Xanax appeared, some 60 million Americans took Valium each year. It, too, turned out to be addictive.

The Drug-naming Process

The naming of prescription and over-the-counter drugs is a complicated process. Each new drug gets three names: chemical, generic, and brand (trademark). Supposedly, this system avoids confusion; for the public, it often creates it.

The chemical name is usually long and hard to pronounce. It tells the molecular structure of the drug, mainly of interest to researchers. When a drug is approved by the FDA, it is assigned

The
First
Miracle
Drug

In 1929, Dr. Alexander Fleming, working in St. Mary's Hospital, London, England, published a paper on a chemical he called penicillin. He said it stopped the growth of germs. But it took until World War II (1939–1945) before further research showed the true importance of Fleming's discovery. Before penicillin, it was not uncommon for people to die from infections that resulted from a mere scratch. Simply put, penicillin stops infection. Today, deaths from infectious bacterial diseases in the United States have markedly declined; they accounted for 797 deaths per 100,000 in 1900 to 59 deaths in 1996—thanks to Dr. Fleming. (*JAMA*, 1999; 281(1):61–6)

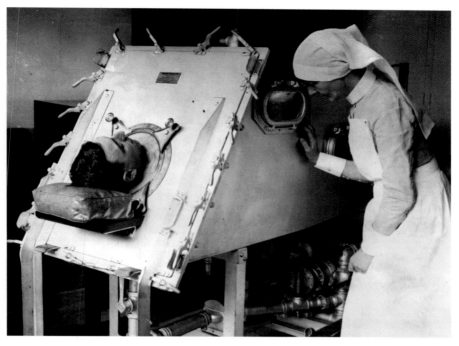

The rise of pharmaceuticals—particularly penicillin—made machines such as the iron lung mercifully obsolete.

a generic (official) name by the United States Adopted Names (USAN) Council. Researchers and those who write about drugs often use the generic name because it refers to the drug itself, not to a company's brand.

The new drug manufacturer or sponsor is the only one that can produce the drug for seventeen years, the length of a new drug patent. The generic name is not owned by the initial manufacturer or sponsor. After the patent runs out, other companies can manufacture the drug under its generic name.

The company that develops the drug gives it a brand or trademark name. This is the name that doctors generally use when describing drugs to patients, and it is the name that most patients use when listing drugs they take. The brand name can be used during the seventeen-year length of the new drug patent.

Unlike the generic name, the brand or trademark name is owned by the manufacturer. In a sense, it's like naming a car or other product. The company wants to attract the attention of the consumer, so brand names are usually not complicated or confusing.

Here are two examples of drug names. Verapamil (generic name) is used to treat irregular heartbeats and high blood pressure. Its brand names are Isoptin, Verelan, Calan, Bosoptin. Its chemical name: 2-(3,4-dimethoxyphenyl)-5-[2-(3,4-dimethoxyphenyl)ethyl-methyl-amino]-2-(1-methylethyl) pentanenitrile. Methyl-phenidate (generic name) is commonly used to treat attention deficit hyperactivity disorder (ADHD) in children. It is marketed under the brand names of Ritalin, Ritalina, Rilatine, Attenta, Methylin, Penid, Rubifen. Its chemical name: Methyl 2-phenyl-2-(piperidin-2-yl)acetate.

Prescription Drugs: A Political Issue

Many people find lots to complain about with the U.S. health-care system. Health insurance is too expensive. It doesn't cover everybody. With some plans, you can't choose your own doctor. It doesn't treat everyone the same. The rich get better treatment . . . and on and on. But if there is one major issue about the system that everyone can agree on, from an unemployed farm worker to a U.S. senator, it is prescription drug coverage. Low-income families may not be able to afford asthma medicines for their children. Retired people may suffer without pills for arthritis pain or skimp on diabetes medications because they cost too much. And, in a strange quirk of the system, those who need drugs the most and can afford them the least often have to pay higher prices for them. That's because people on Medicare who don't have supplementary insurance, such as AARP, are charged higher prices by the drug industry than, say, preferred customers such as the Veterans Administration (VA). And that's because the VA can buy in bulk. The average insurance owner simply doesn't have any bargaining clout.

Drug companies are a powerful lobby in Washington, D.C. According to a *USA Today* article by a spokesperson for National Women's Health Network, "They are one of the strongest, most well-connected and most effective lobbies in Washington. Going up against them is more often than not a losing battle."

The job of lobbyists is to promote the interests of their companies. That job is often made easier by their connections. For instance, in 2004, twenty-six lobbyists for drug companies reportedly were former members of Congress. One might well assume that they had a sympathetic ear in the government. Drug companies also contribute handsomely to political campaigns. For instance, they gave almost $1 million to George W. Bush's second campaign in 2004 and nearly $500,000 to his opponent, John Kerry. All this influence works. The drug industry has been successful in stopping imports of cheaper medicines from Canada and other countries. They won coverage for prescription drugs under Medicare in 2003. That stopped Medicare from using its huge purchasing power to bargain for low prices.

Drug companies want deep connections within the government because they are so dependent on federal decisions. The government buys massive quantities of drugs via programs such as Medicaid and the Veterans Administration. And it is the government that decides what drugs can go on the market and how they can be labeled.

Because of the industry's power and the products it sells, there are more and more calls for reform. For instance, Senators Chuck Grassley of Iowa and Chris Dodd of Connecticut are pushing for laws requiring that all data on clinical trials of a new medicine be released. (Drug companies don't like to give out negative results.) In her book, *The Truth About the Drug Companies*, Dr. Marcia Angell, former editor-in-chief of the *New England Journal of Medicine*, argues the FDA should be made stronger. She says that government regulations have weakened the FDA as a watchdog over the drug companies. She also believes that drug companies should not be in charge of the clinical testing of their own drugs. Instead, such testing should be supervised by a separate institute, perhaps within the National Institutes of Health.

Teen Abuse of Prescription Drugs

Prescription drug abuse is on the rise—especially among teenagers. According to the Partnership for a Drug-Free America, "1 in 5 teens has abused a prescription pain medication; 1 in 5 report abusing prescription stimulants and tranquilizers; 1 in 10 has abused cough medication." So-called pharm parties are popular. Many different pills are thrown together in a bowl, and the resulting "trail mix" is then passed around. The users have no idea what they're taking.

The popular novel and movie, *Valley of the Dolls,* was a graphic representation of the blatant misuse of prescription medication during the 1960s. It was very popular with teens.

Should Cold Medicines Be Illegal?

A front-page article in the *Journal News* of Westchester County, New York, April 21, 2008, concerned a fourteen-year-old boy. The school nurse called his mother because his blood pressure was sky-high and he was, as the nurse said, "out of it." After a visit to the doctor, the boy admitted that he had swallowed fifty liquid gel caps of a common cold medicine. Why? To get high.

This practice among teens and "tweens" is called robo-tripping. It means using over-the-counter cold medicines, such as Robitussin, to get high. According to the article, ten teenagers in the county had landed in the hospital since the beginning of the year for overdosing on cold medicines. The ingredient that can bring on out-of-body sensations is the cough suppressant known as DXM. In large amounts, DXM can cause high blood pressure, vomiting, seizures, and even death. County lawmakers are considering a limit on the sale of medicines containing DXM. They also suggest that parents lock their medicine cabinets.

Many teens think that if a drug has been prescribed by a doctor, perhaps to kill the pain of a knee injury, it must be okay for other uses—like getting high. The truth is that drugs taken without a specific prescription or used for other than the stated purpose can be just as dangerous as cocaine or any other narcotic. They can also be just as addictive.

Prescription drugs are vital, necessary, and generally safe when they are taken as directed. They help to ease depression. They treat ADHD. They deaden the pain of a football injury. But if these same drugs are taken by someone who isn't depressed, doesn't have ADHD, and isn't injured, they can become something else. It's called drug abuse.

Prescription drug abuse is dangerous. These drugs are safe only for the people who have prescriptions for them and who take them according to a doctor's instructions. A doctor who writes a prescription has presumably examined the patient and tried to rule out a bad reaction to the drug. The patient may also be warned to avoid such things as drinking alcohol or taking another drug while on the medication.

Prescription drug abuse is not only as dangerous as abusing street drugs, it's also just as illegal. Those who take a drug without a prescription or share a prescription drug with friends are breaking the law.

Why do people abuse prescription drugs? Besides the fact that some wrongly believe them to be safe, the truth is, they're available. Usually they sit right on the shelf of the family medicine cabinet, and who keeps track? Raiding the medicine cabinet is easier than arranging a cocaine sale—and a lot cheaper. Three types of prescription drugs are commonly abused: depressants, opiates, and stimulants. Central nervous system (CNS) depressants reduce tension and anxiety and improve sleep. They work by slowing down brain activity, which makes a person calm or drowsy. There are two types of depressants: barbiturates, such as pentobarbital sodium (Nembutal), and benzodiazepines, such as diazepam (Valium). Opiates such as meperidine (Demerol) are prescribed for pain. They attach to receptors in the brain and spinal cord and stop pain signals from reaching the brain. Stimulants are used in the treatment of ADHD and depression. Such drugs as methylphenidate (Ritalin) boost brain activity, which results in more energy and alertness.

There is danger in taking any of these drugs without a prescription. Too many stimulants can cause an irregular heartbeat. Depressants mixed with other drugs can slow the heart so much that it stops. And even if there are no side effects, what does happen with prescription drug abuse is the same thing that happens with street drug abuse: addiction. That means the user is hooked. The user's body craves this particular drug or substance. It can change his or her mood, outlook, weight, and certainly his or her life. Here's a simple-but-smart rule to follow: A person should never, ever take any prescription drug that hasn't been prescribed just for him or her.

6 Health-care Services Worldwide

FACT: Americans have a lower life expectancy (70.0 years)
than other industrialized nations with universal
health care, such as Australia (73.2 years).
—DALE, Disability Adjusted Life Expectancy, a system
developed by WHO that counted babies born in 1999.

GOVERNMENT PROGRAMS THAT GIVE ALL CITIZENS
free or subsidized access to health care are known as universal
health-care programs. Most of the cost is paid by taxes and/or

**The clarion call for health care for all was thought to be part of what caused
President Obama to win the 2008 election.**

compulsory health insurance. Some patients may pay some part of their care directly. Most developed and many developing nations provide universal health care to their citizens. The United States does not. How successful are these health-care systems? What are the drawbacks? Can any of these methods be applied to improving the U.S. system?

The World Health Organization (WHO) ranks nations of the world according to their health-care systems, based on such factors as quality and availability of care, who is covered, and costs. See the chart for rankings and statistics of the nations covered.

HEALTH STATISTICS

Country	WHO Ranking	Population (2007)	Life Expectancy (in years)
Canada	30	32,876,000	81
Costa Rica	36	4,468,000	79
Cuba	40	11,268,000	78
France	1	61,647,000	81
Germany	25	82,599,000	79
Great Britain	18	60,769,000	72
Iran	93	71,208,000	71
Israel	28	6,928,000	81
Japan	10	127,967,000	83
Russian Federation	130	142,499,000	66
United States	37	305,826,000	78

Source: *New York Times Almanac,* 2008.

Canada

Public funds pay for Canada's health system and private facilities provide the services. Canadians took some steps toward universal care in the early twentieth century. However, various attempts to set up a nationwide system failed. Finally, in 1946, Saskatchewan passed the Saskatchewan Hospitalization Act. The province had suffered from a shortage of medical aid for many years, even creating a program in which a town could pay a doctor to practice there. The 1946 law gave free hospital care to most of Saskatchewan's citizens. Alberta province followed with a similar plan in 1950. Seven years later, the federal government passed the Hospital Insurance and Diagnostic Services (HIDS) Act. It paid half the cost of health programs in the ten provinces and three territories that make up the nation of Canada.

Universal health care actually began in 1966 with the Medical Care Act. It allowed each province to set up a universal plan, and it established the Medicare system. In 1984, the Canada Health Act was passed. That stopped user fees and extra billing by doctors. There are many variations across the country concerning home and long-term care and prescription drugs.

About 70 percent of Canadian health care is paid for by the government, including doctor visits and ER treatment. The largest such program is Medicare, which consists of separate programs in each of the provinces. The federal government pays direct health-care costs for military personnel and for prison inmates. It also assumes responsibility for First Nations. These are native peoples, most of whom use the regular hospitals, although some are served by clinics on reservations.

The remaining 30 percent of health care in Canada is funded privately, usually to pay for prescription drugs and dental needs. Most Canadians have private health insurance, often paid by their employers. Doctors generally are not paid an annual salary but charge per visit.

Canada spends about 10 percent of its GNP on health care as opposed to about 15 percent in the United States. Drug prices in Canada are lower, although they have been rising in recent years.

According to an article in the *San Francisco Chronicle*, "while Americans value the quality of U.S. health care, 62 percent think the nation should shift to a universal health insurance program like Canada's." But are there drawbacks to the Canadian system? Yes, there are, continued the article: "The health system is now itself in need of emergency care in order to continue offering the benefits Canadians have come to think of as their birthright."

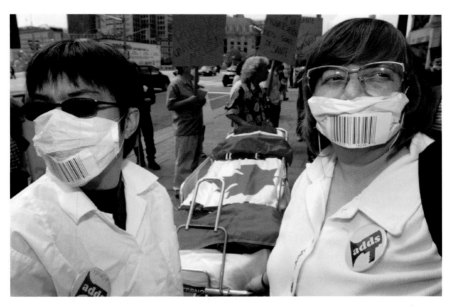

Though many criticize the long waiting times to see a physician in Canada, many more want it to remain a right, not a privilege. Here two women wear surgical masks with bar codes in front of a gurney with a Canadian flag blanket to protest the privatization of Canada's health-care system.

One problem seems to be waiting time. According to the Fraser Institute, a Canadian research and educational organization, Canadians wait about eighteen weeks on average for surgical and other therapeutic treatment. They often wait hours in emergency rooms; Americans wait an hour on average for ER treatment. A hip replacement might mean a wait of two years. The Canadian Medical Association blasted one of the provinces with this headline: "Saskatchewan's 22-Month Wait for an MRI is 'Almost Criminal' Says Radiologists' Association." It cited a lack of MRI machines as the main problem. According to the report, at the time some 4,500 people in the province were waiting for an MRI. In 2007, the Canadian government promised shorter waiting times within three years.

Canada's health care is also plagued by high costs that drain the system, and by a shortage of doctors. To correct these complaints, the government has pledged more money. It also plans to train more physicians and to make it easier for foreign doctors to practice in Canada. Like the United States, the country also faces swiftly rising prescription drug prices and a population that lives longer and therefore uses the health-care system for longer periods. But even with these problems, Canadians overwhelmingly say they are in favor of their health-care program.

Costa Rica

The Republic of Costa Rica is about the size of the state of West Virginia. It has universal health care and one of the best health systems in Latin America. It also has the usual red tape and long waits. However, citizens have access to private health care that is high quality and affordable.

Health care is paid for by the government. The Caja Costarricense de Seguro Social (CCSS, the Costa Rican social security system) is responsible for providing low-cost care in the 30 hospitals and more than 250 clinics. Affordable health care extends to noncitizens as well. Foreigners who live there pay a small monthly fee, based on income, to join the CCSS, or they buy insurance from the state. Doctors often work for the CCSS in the mornings and operate clinics in the afternoons and evenings.

Magnetic Resonance Imaging

The MRI is a non-X-ray diagnostic tool that has been in use since the 1980s. It can take pictures of almost all tissues in the human body. The patient lies inside a large magnet that is shaped like a cylinder. As the patient passes through the cylinder, strong radio waves are sent through the body. They go back and forth and make radio waves of their own. The radio waves become pictures that show any problems, such as tumors. The MRI does not expose the patient to X-rays or other radiation and it is painless. (The radiation effects of X-rays can cause damage to living tissue, such as tissue in the bones called bone marrow.) Many patients, however, report feelings of claustrophobia inside the cylinder. For those, some facilities offer the open MRI, in which there is more open space around the body.

Two first-class, ultramodern private hospitals, Clínica Bíblica and Clínica Católica, are affiliated with hospitals in the United States. Their charges are higher than public facilities but lower than any such U.S. facility.

Cuba

The island of Cuba has a long history of medical care, with the first surgical clinic established in 1823. With the revision of the Cuban constitution in 1976, all citizens have the right to health care. Almost universal vaccinations were started in the 1960s and many contagious diseases have been eradicated or greatly reduced. In 1970, a program was initiated to reduce the infant mortality rate; in 2007 Cuba announced it would start to computerize and create national networks in blood banks and medical imaging. These improvements have been implemented at a comparatively low cost.

Cuba started a program of training doctors, inviting many students from the Caribbean area, Latin America, African and Middle Eastern countries, and even a few from the United States. The graduates are asked to return to their home countries and work in poorly served areas for a period of time as their medical education payment.

Following the end of Soviet subsidies in the 1990s, and as a result of the continuing U.S. trade embargo, Cuba's medical care experienced shortages of supplies. However, life expectancy is now comparable to that in the United States and, according to WHO, Cuba is second only to Italy in doctor-to-patient ratio with a doctor for every 170 residents. Another indicator of health is the literacy rate. Cuba's is 96.4, indicating a link between education and good health care. However, difficulty in obtaining certain medicines or treatments on the island has led to an increasing role of the black market in providing health care. There have been reports of patients being charged "under the table" for quicker or better service.

France

WHO ranks health care in the French Republic as the best in the world. The system's success is seen in the high life expectancy rate of eighty-one years. Everyone who is salaried is covered by the national health plan known as *sécurité sociale* (social security). That includes spouses and children of the workers. Those who are not workers take out special coverage, called *l'assurance personnelle* (personal, or individual, insurance). In 2000, the government passed the CMU (*couverture maladie universelle*, or universal medical coverage) plan, covering those who have been residents for at least three months. Anyone not covered by the basic national health plan must enroll in CMU.

Health services are funded by indirect taxes on alcohol and tobacco and by direct taxes paid by workers according to income, much like social security taxes in the United States. Most health expenses are paid for, but much of the population also has supplemental insurance from their employers to cover small copayments. Those who cannot afford that insurance, however, still get free universal care.

French citizens can choose from a variety of doctors, specialists, and hospitals, regardless of patient income. There are three types of facilities in the system: public hospitals, private clinics, and nonprofit care. Public hospitals include local, general, and university institutions. The Public Assistance Hospital of Paris, created after the French Revolution in the late eighteenth century, sets standards of care for the country. All those who work in public hospitals are paid as hospital practitioners.

Private clinics were started by French doctors. Since 1991, they are required to share any medical files with colleagues in other facilities. Nonprofit health care is funded by endowments, as are public hospitals. They make up about 14 percent of health care in the system.

But all of this service comes at a high cost. The French system is among the most expensive in the world. It takes up nearly 10 percent of the GNP. High costs are blamed on overuse of prescription drugs and waste within the system itself. Even so, most citizens approve of their health services. They boast that waiting lines for surgery do not exist in France as they do in other nations with universal health care.

Germany

All 82 million citizens of the Federal Republic of Germany are covered by health-care plans. Until the age of sixty-five, they must pay into health insurance plans that are state-regulated or private. Most have state plans; the self-employed and those who earn about four thousand U.S. dollars a month can take out private plans. Payments stop after retirement age but coverage continues until death. The German system boasts that waiting times for health services are rare, although there may be some minor delays for nonemergency surgery.

State-regulated plans include in-house services for workers in large companies. A plan called *Ersatzkassen* covers smaller firms and blue-collar workers. The poor and the unemployed are covered by the state. State plans take about 14 percent of a worker's gross income yearly. Private insurance is also state regulated. Those eligible for private insurance include the self-employed, public workers such as teachers and the police, and those with high incomes. The government tries to discourage private insurance since it loses the money it collects when workers pay for the state plans. All types of insurance cover doctor and hospital fees, long-term care, and some dental services.

Doctors who work in hospitals are employed by them. Those in private practice are self-employed, work out of their own offices, and refer patients to hospitals when necessary.

Despite its record, health care in Germany is not without its critics. Malpractice suits have increased over the past few years. The government has put strict limits on hospital expenses. Some fear this may cause hospital workers to leave the country for more lucrative jobs. Ambulatory services could be improved, and there are few facilities in the country for breast cancer screening.

These deficiencies worry some Germans. According to an article on health care, many Germans look on the system "as being in a crisis and fear that it is turning into a 'two-class' system whereby the rich would be able to buy private, comprehensive, quality healthcare but those legally bound to the state-regulated schemes would receive only basic healthcare."

Great Britain

The National Health Service (NHS) has been in operation in the United Kingdom since 1948. Every U.K. resident is covered by a system funded only through income tax and run by the Department of Health. It is the world's largest health service and one of the largest employers in the world. In fact, in an article for the *Telegraph* in 2005, John Hibbs, head of news for NHS, ranked it this way: "You may be interested to know that our best intelligence suggests our world ranking is as follows: Chinese People's Liberation Army . . . , U.S. Dept. of Defence . . . , Indian Railways . . . , Walmart. So that makes the NHS . . . at least fifth largest in the world—if you don't count McDonalds."

The NHS is divided into primary and secondary care services administered by local NHS organizations called trusts. There are about three hundred primary trusts in England. They cover such services as general doctors, dentists, pharmacists, opticians, and others. The trusts decide what health services are needed in an area and have the responsibility to make sure they are available. Primary care trusts can also employ private companies for services.

Secondary care, delivered by various other NHS trusts, covers services including hospitals, mental health problems, and ambulances. Private facilities are often used for seeing a dermatologist, for instance, or for cosmetic surgery.

Less than 10 percent of Great Britain's population uses private health care, which is paid for by insurance or when people use the services. There are, however, about three hundred private hospitals in Great Britain funded by private groups. They are licensed by the local health-care officials but not regulated by the inspectors who monitor NHS facilities. Private funds also supply some services within the NHS. But, as of a government contract change in 2006, dental services in the NHS are not as available as they once were.

The NHS is unique among European systems in two ways. It pays directly for health expenses, and it employs nearly all the hospital doctors and nurses in England. Primary doctors, dentists, and other providers are usually self-employed and have contracts with the NHS.

A number of agencies make sure that British citizens get good care. The National Institute for Clinical Excellence (NICE) publishes guidelines on disease and medical devices, which the NHS is supposed to follow. Private hospitals are not required to do so. The General Medical Council protects citizens from medical malpractice. The Health Service Ombudsman investigates patient complaints. The National Patient Safety Agency makes sure safety standards are followed.

For all its rules and regulations, the NHS has long been the target of criticism. Since the NHS offers free coverage to almost every citizen, it must sometimes ration its services. A heart attack victim takes priority over someone waiting to have a benign cyst (noncancerous growth) removed. As in many universal systems around the world, a major complaint is waiting time. And wait people do, sometimes for months. In response to criticism, the

NHS has said it aims to make all waiting times no more than eighteen weeks. Another problem not unique to the British system is the rising cost of medical care and prescription drugs. Taxpayers who buy private health-care insurance argue that they are paying twice since they still contribute to NHS through their taxes. That criticism, however, is always present when there are existing public and private funds for services.

Iran

The Islamic Republic of Iran, a densely populated country in the Middle East, has about seventy-one million people. According to its constitution, Iranians are entitled to basic health-care services. The Ministry of Health and Medical Education operates general hospitals, as well as specialty hospitals for those with higher incomes. Public clinics serve those with limited funds.

Since the revolution of 1979, most Iranians have some access to health care. There have been many advances in medical technology. However, health services continue to be scarce in the rural areas. Communicable diseases such as cholera remain a problem, mostly because there are few facilities for treating wastewater in the country. In the capital city of Tehran, for example, in many areas raw sewage goes right into the groundwater. As Iran's population increases, so do the health risks because of this water pollution problem. Life expectancy for males is sixty-eight years; for females it is seventy-one years.

Israel

Health care in Israel is ranked twenty-eighth by the World Health Organization. By the time Israel became an independent nation in 1948, a public-health system was already active. Mother and child care centers offered services, and government-funded health insurance provided doctor and specialist care. The system is based on health-maintenance organizations (HMOs) that were originally set up by labor unions. A 1973 law mandated that employers must provide medical insurance for their workers.

In 1995, the government enacted the National Health Insurance Law. Every Israeli citizen must be insured by one of four health funds according to his or her choice. The law set up a list of medical services to be provided by the health funds. They are paid for by a tax on income (up to 4.8 percent) and by employer contributions. Israel spends more than 8 percent of its GNP on health services.

Israeli citizens have access to a large number of hospitals, both general and specialized. The state and the Clalit HMO have the biggest general hospitals in the country, including the Tel Aviv Medical Center in Tel Aviv and Carmel Hospital in Haifa.

Health care in Israel benefits from the Master of Public Health (MPH) course begun by the Hadassah Braun School of Public and Community Medicine, part of Hebrew University. It trains public health workers and researchers. Graduates of these programs form the basis for the nation's health care. Israel also has four medical schools (all university-affiliated), two dental schools, and twenty nursing schools for a population of approximately 6 million. Most of the country's doctors are salaried by the hospitals. Israel has one of the highest doctor-to-patient ratios in the world with more than four physicians to every one thousand people.

The Israel Council for Public Health runs campaigns to keep citizens aware of health hazards. In this way, smoking has been reduced, malaria and diphtheria have been wiped out, and the country has the lowest number of new HIV cases in the Western world. Heart disease and cancer are the largest killers, as is true in most Western nations.

Despite the success of its health system, services in Israel suffer from common problems. The population is aging, which puts a drain on facilities and services. And medical services and equipment are increasingly expensive. The government is trying to combat these problems with increased research. For instance, a study showed that most patients get better more quickly if they can recover outside the hospital. Shorter stays led to a reduction in hospital beds, thereby saving money.

Japan

Japan's universal care requires coverage by either National Health Insurance or Employees' Health Insurance. National Health covers those who are self-employed or not employed, such as retired persons, students, expectant mothers, or workers in the fishing, forestry, or agriculture industries. Coverage includes illness or injury, dental services, and death of the insured or dependents. Not covered are cosmetic surgeries, abortions, injuries resulting from intoxication, and medical services taken outside the country.

Employees' Health Insurance covers workers in medium and large companies, in government, and private schools. A separate plan takes care of small businesses. Premiums for both insurance plans are about 4 percent of the insured's salary. A program that covers the elderly—those over seventy—is funded by both plans.

Efficient as it is, Japan's system suffers from many of the ills of other industrialized countries. It is increasingly expensive. For instance, hospital stays in Japan are generally two or three times longer than in Western countries. As a result, Japan needs many more hospital beds, which are costly. Medical experts warn of other problems for health care in Japan, mainly that elderly retirees will soon outnumber young working citizens. How can that smaller number support so many older citizens?

Russia

The Russian Federation, or Russia, is the largest of the states that once formed the Soviet Union (USSR). WHO ranks its health care a dismal 130 out of the 190 countries on its list. According to a report from the Voice of America, the official radio/TV broadcasting service of the U.S. federal government: "In the last decade, the health of the average Russian has grown significantly worse. . . . The three major causes of illness among Russians are respiratory disease, circulatory disorders, and alcohol-related injury and poisoning. . . . Yet, despite these alarming trends, public health has not been high on the government's agenda."

Under Joseph Stalin, in office from 1927 to 1953, the Russian system of socialized medicine promised free health care to all citizens. The USSR (Union of Soviet Socialist Republics) was established in 1921 and lasted until 1992. It was the world's largest country, covering more than eight million square miles and including fourteen separate republics in addition to Russia itself. By the 1980s, people in all the republics were covered by local and work-site clinics all over the vast union. Large hospital complexes were available to most. This huge, multilevel operation was directed from Moscow. All programs were given goals to reach. Much of the allotted funds were spent each year on new facilities.

But by the mid-1990s, the Soviet Union had collapsed. The republics were independent countries once again. The health-care system in Russia began to collapse as well. The Russian people still have free basic health care, but it is of poor quality and mismanaged, says the Heartland Institute, a public policy nonprofit organization based in Chicago. The country spends about 3 percent of its GNP on health services compared to about 10 percent in France and 15 percent in the United States.

Many factors contributed to the decline in Russian health care, such as contamination from nuclear accidents, overcrowded living conditions, a high rate of alcoholism, and a lack of new technology. The structure of the system itself also contributed to the fall. A specified treatment length was given to every illness or disease.

As a result, a person with even a relatively light case of the flu, for instance, might be hospitalized instead of recovering at home. Hospital overcrowding was soon a fact. Poorly trained and poorly paid personnel hastened the decline. It was reported that about half of the country's doctors could not read an electrocardiogram (a graph of heart activity) when they graduated from medical school.

In 2006, the Russian government decided to take action. It announced it would increase spending on health care by taking funds mainly from oil revenues. The new plan called for high-tech medical centers, new equipment, and salary increases for doctors and nurses. It also shifted the emphasis from how *many* people were treated to how *well* they were treated.

Although Russia's deputy health minister called these changes of great benefit to the people, others had doubts. Commented Sergei Smirnov, head of the Institute of Social Policies and Social-Economic Programs: "How is it possible . . . that a national health care project is managed not by the health ministry but by the presidential administration?"

7 Where Are We Going?

FACT: Health care advocates need to develop a "template" that
doesn't compromise core health care principles but one that also
can win the political support needed to be enacted.
—Jacob Hacker, Yale University economist, 2008

WHERE ARE WE GOING WITH HEALTH CARE IN
America? Sometimes it seems like nowhere. Any proposals
for setting up a universal health plan have been rejected. Why?
As noted in a *New Yorker* article by Malcom Gladwell, "One of
the great mysteries of political life in the United States is why
Americans are so devoted to their health-care system . . . the United
States has opted for a makeshift system of increasing complexity
and dysfunction." After citing the fact that Americans spend more
money on health care than any other nation, Gladwell asks: "What
does that extra spending buy us? Americans have fewer doctors per
capita than most Western countries." And if that were not enough:
"American life expectancy is lower than the Western average." The
mystery continues.

Baby Boomers

Health care in America seems to have reached a crisis in large part
due to the so-called Baby Boomers, which refers to people born
between 1946 and 1964, give or take a few years. Following World
War II, there was an unusual spike in the country's birth rate. Now,

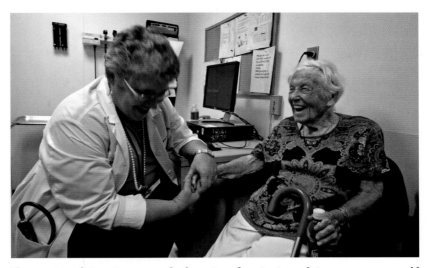

The graying of America means the booming of geriatric medicine, or so one would think. In fact, few young medical students are interested in that specialty.

according to estimates, about 78 million Baby Boomers are nearing retirement age. The oldest of them will celebrate their sixty-fifth birthdays in 2011.

More and more, the Baby Boomers will need health-care services. Today, about 17 percent of Americans are aged sixty-five and older. By 2030, about 26 percent of the population will be sixty-five and older. But there is more involved here than sheer numbers. In earlier years, many older Americans relied on their families to care for them in retirement years. That is largely no longer true. When the Baby Boomers were born, U.S. families were more apt to be living close together. There were fewer divorces and more children. Also, the kinds of care are different today than yesterday. If a man survived a severe heart attack in the 1950s, for instance, the "cure" was probably bed rest for a few months and limited activity thereafter, which was probably not very long. Today, the same severe attack will likely be treated with surgery to repair clogged arteries and drugs to regulate blood flow. The result may well be a longer and more active life . . . but the treatment is expensive.

Support Programs

As the U.S. population grows older and lives longer, health-care providers are trying to meet some of their needs by reaching out to the families and friends of older adults. An example is the Family Caregiver Support Program in Westchester County, New York, through the Department of Senior Programs and Services. The county has five full-service centers, including an Alzheimers Association, and twelve resource centers in county libraries. The program includes spring and fall workshops that educate caregivers in available services throughout the county, a quarterly newsletter with important data for caregivers, and a staff that invites the caregiver to call or come in to talk about the problems of caring for the elderly. Also included is help with a serious problem for many caregivers: what to do when an older driver insists on getting behind the wheel of a car. Other support programs in Westchester include a group for seniors older than sixty who are raising grandchildren of eighteen years or younger.

In addition, Baby Boomers simply expect more. Senior Americans today often don't accept the old adage that pain or infirmity is a natural part of aging. They want medicines or services that will keep them active and reasonably healthy well into their late years. By and large, this is not a let's-grow-old-and-act-our-age group.

Faced with these prospects, it seems obvious that the current U.S. health force cannot meet the requirements and expectations of aging Americans and at the same time take care of all others in medical need. Says John W. Rowe of the Mailman School of Public Health in New York: "We face an impending crisis as the growing number of older patients, who are living longer with more complex health needs, increasingly outpaces the number of health-care providers with the knowledge and skills to care for them capably." What to do?

Some health-care providers are planning now. The American Geriatrics Society says that more than 30,000 geriatricians will be needed by 2028. A geriatrician is a doctor especially trained to care for the health needs of older adults. The Summa Health System in Akron, Ohio, for instance, now offers two fellowship programs to train doctors of geriatrics. In partnership with the Cleveland Clinic, the program gives a year of clinical training and an optional year of research. Recognizing the growing need for future nursing services, DeKalb Medical in Georgia held a career fair for nurses in April 2008. It promised that all qualified candidates would get an interview and possibly a job. DeKalb listed the starting salary for new nurses at $47,000.

The real problem for health-care providers may be a shortage of primary-care physicians. Medical education costs, plus a desire for a better lifestyle, often lead medical school graduates into specialties in medicine, which pay more and tend to have better working hours. This trend makes it more difficult for patients to find primary-care doctors who, in turn, help them make better health-care choices. Some suggest opening medical schools to

Sick
or
Sicko?

In 2007, filmmaker Michael Moore got the attention of the American public—and certainly the medical field—with his blast at U.S. health care. It was one of the most talked-about productions at the Cannes Film Festival in France that year. In a not-very-subtle presentation, *Sicko* deals with what Moore and many others feel are the real failings of the U.S. health-care system. It especially focuses on for-profit health insurance and the pharmaceutical industry. It shows victims of insurance company fraud and red tape. It interviews people denied care even though they thought they were covered by insurance. It speaks of HMO practices in a less than flattering way. And it compares the U.S. system unfavorably to those in Canada, Cuba, and notably France. *Sicko* got its share of praise and everyone's attention. It also got its share of criticism by those who claim Moore exaggerated and misrepresented many aspects of the U.S. health system.

larger enrollments and focusing on primary care as a key part of the overall U.S. health-care system.

Some experts in the medical field point to unhealthy lifestyle choices as the true culprit in our health-care problems. For one thing, Americans are just too fat. Obesity drives up the costs of health care. The American Heart Association estimates that about 60 percent of Americans are overweight or obese. Overweight children and adults are at risk for heart disease, high blood pressure, high cholesterol, and type 2 diabetes. All those conditions are expensive to treat and control.

Other health problems that drive up the price of health care in America are heart disease, cancer, and stroke. These chronic diseases, along with injuries, are the leading killers, and most health-care money goes into high-tech cures and techniques.

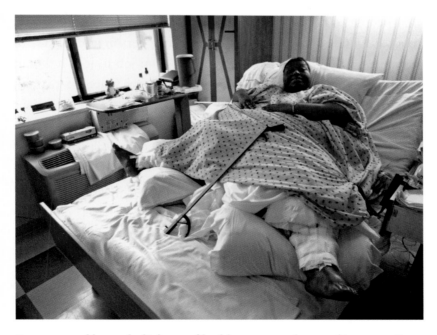

Not everyone blames the high cost of health care on an absence of insurance. Some believe that problems such as obesity—the fastest-rising major health problem in the United States—are the real culprits.

New Ideas

In the twenty-first century, there are renewed—and louder—cries for U.S. health-care reform. Both presidential candidates in the 2008 election promised to end the crisis. While running for office, President Barack Obama proposed a plan of health insurance for almost all Americans—and *all* children—regardless of medical history, creating a national public insurance program. People can also buy into government-offered insurance. Insurance will be affordable to lower-income Americans. But the plan that President Obama presented does not mandate that everyone must have insurance. He has, though, made reform of the health-care field and the extension of insurance a high priority.

Republican candidate John McCain's plan would have set up a tax credit worth as much as five thousand dollars per family per year to buy health insurance. It would not, however, have guaranteed that people could get insurance, but it would have been available to all and not limited by income or where a person works. Health insurance would have followed a person from job to job. It would have stayed in effect if the person took a few years off to raise children.

Other members of Congress have also proposed changes to U.S. health care. In 2007, for instance, Senator Chris Dodd of Connecticut, while campaigning for the Democratic presidential nomination, announced his universal health plan. Phased in over four years, it would build an insurance package for both individuals and businesses based on ability to pay. Called Universal HealthMart, it is similar to the current plan for federal workers. Dodd said it would be paid for mainly by cutting out the waste in the current system.

Senator Ron Wyden of Oregon proposed the Healthy Americans Act. It guarantees health coverage for everyone in a plan similar to that for congressional members. Employers would not pay for health coverage. Instead, that cost would be given as extra salary,

President Obama came into office on a platform that included extending affordable health-care insurance to as many people as possible. It will take some time before that platform can become reality.

which the employees would be required to use for health insurance. Families earning between $40,000 and $50,000 a year would pay about $81 yearly. Those who earn up to $150,000 would pay about $327 a year. Whatever the shape of health-care reform, it seems assured that there will be a change in the next four to eight years.

Congressional Health Care for Everyone?

Members of Congress belong to a group of Americans who rarely complain about health care. All of them, plus more than nine million other federal employees and retirees, are covered by the Federal Employees Health Benefits Program (FEHBP), created in 1959. Some lawmakers, including former senator John Breaux of Louisiana and Representative Connie Mack of Florida, have at one time discussed Medicare reform similar to the key features of FEHBP.

The congressional care system is run by a small bureaucracy that does not set prices for doctors and hospitals, unlike Medicare. Members have a choice of several health plans in each city, including HMOs and preferred-provider programs. They choose a plan that suits them, the government pays most of the cost, and the members pay the rest. In a basic plan, the premium is small. For more expensive plans, the fees are naturally higher. The congressional plan is able to keep costs down while improving benefits.

The key features of FEHBP are:

- Premium costs are kept under control;
- Premiums are negotiated instead of paying a rigid formula;
- Many private plans compete;
- A good information system keeps members informed of good choices in health plans;
- Premiums and benefits are negotiated between the Office of Personnel Management, which runs the FEHBP, and the individual plans;
- The staff that runs the FEHBP is small, keeping costs down;
- There is no bidding to determine which plans can or can't compete for members.

For all its benefits, the FEHBP is not without critics, who cite two problems. They complain of an outdated system of insurance underwriting, meaning those who assess the risks of covering a potential client. The other problem is adverse selection. That refers to the tendency of people with high-risk health needs to apply for insurance more than those who have lesser health risks.

Could the congressional system work for everyone? Some experts think so. Says Robert E. Moffit, director of The Heritage Foundation's Center for Health Policy Studies: "To replicate the FEHBP, all you have to do is let Americans pick and choose their health care plans nationwide. . . . So in New Hampshire and New Jersey, where health insurance premiums are high, people could then have the choice to pick a cheaper plan in Iowa. . . . With a national market for health insurance, you would have the same dynamics in play that are there for federal employees. And with large national pools, you would have lower administration costs."

But not everyone agrees. Devon Herrick at the National Center for Policy Analysis says: "I think one reason why the FEHBP works for the federal government is because they have so much buying power, yet aren't so big that they can take over the whole market. . . . For the most part, federal employees are healthy and tend to be in pretty good shape. And because the group they are underwriting is so large, they are able to squeeze the price and make things more affordable."

With all the ideas and suggestions, the crazy quilt is still in place. Health-care premiums continue to rise at about four times the rate of the average American's income, according to experts. The United States is still the only major country to look upon health care for its citizens as a service to be purchased rather than as a universal right. Most everyone agrees that the U.S. health-care system is in need of change. Most Americans want more and better choices. But they don't want them at the cost of higher prices. Is that possible? It seems that everyone recognizes the problems. Yet, the debate goes on.

Notes

Introduction

p. 6, "According to the survey . . . ": "Most Republicans Think the U.S. Health Care System is the Best in the World. Democrats Disagree," Harvard School of Public Health press release, March 20, 2008, http://www.scienceblog.com/cms/republicans-think-us-health-care-system-best-world-democrats-disagree-15714.html (accessed June 24, 2008).

Chapter 1

p. 7, "The percentage of Americans . . .": Steven Reinberg, "Record Number of Americans Lack Health Insurance," *U.S. News & World Report,* August 8, 2007.

p. 10, "In the United States . . .": Carmen DeNavas-Walt, Bernadette D. Proctor, and Jessica Smith, "Income Poverty and Health Insurance Coverage in the United States: 2006," U.S. Census Bureau, August 2007.

p. 12, "those paying such an extra fee . . .": Vasilios J. Kalogredis, "Should you consider concierge medicine?" *Physician's News Digest,* February 2004, 4.

p. 17, "A well-known example . . .": National Cancer Institute Fact Sheet, February 2008.

p. 20, "nearly 5 million . . .": John W. Wright, ed., *New York Times Almanac* (New York: Penguin, 2008), 376.

Chapter 2

p. 32, "was $2 trillion . . .": "Health Insurance Costs," National Coalition on Health Care, http://www.nchc.org/facts/cost.shtml (accessed February 4, 2008).

p. 32, "Fewer employees receive health insurance . . .": "Employers shift health insurance costs onto workers," Economic Snapshots, Economic Policy Institute, August 16, 2006.

p. 32, "Covered workers . . .": "Health Insurance Premiums Rise 6.1 Percent in 2007, Less Rapidly than in Recent Years But Still Faster than Wages and Inflation," Kaiser Family Foundation news release, September 11, 2007, http://www.kff.org/insurance/ehbs091107nr.cfm (accessed February 7, 2008).

p. 39, "But adverse publicity . . .": Jerry Avorn, *Powerful Medicines* (New York: Knopf, 2004), 231.

p. 45, "That's especially needed . . .": Amy Snow Landa, "Medicaid to offer HAS pilot program," *American Medical News,* March 13, 2006, www.pnhp.org/news/2006/march/medicaids_health_op.php (accessed February 19, 2008).

p. 46, "An estimated 26.2 percent . . .": R. C. Kessler et al., "Prevalence, Severity, and Comorbidity of 12-Month *DSM-IV* Disorders in the National Comorbidity Survey Replication," *Archives of General Psychiatry,* 62, no. 6 (June 2006): 617–627.

p. 46, "after a decade of delays . . .": Rick Weiss, "Study: U.S. Leads in Mental Illness, Lags in Treatment," *Washington Post,* June 7, 2005.

Chapter 3

p. 56, "25 years later . . .": Carol Ballentine, "Taste of Raspberries, Taste of Death," *FDA Consumer,* June 1981, 6.

p. 59, "FDA Says It Approved . . .": Marc Kauman, "FDA Says It Approved the Wrong Drug Plant," *Washington Post,* February 19, 2008.

Chapter 4

p. 70, "Her 2006 study concluded . . .": Gardiner Harris, "Cigarette Company Paid for Lung Cancer Study, " *New York Times*, March 26, 2008.

p. 70, "small print at the end . . .": Harris, "Cigarette Company Paid for Lung Cancer Study."

p. 70, "blood money": Harris, "Cigarette Company Paid for Lung Cancer Study."

p. 71, "one in three Americans . . .": Hans Kuttner and Matthew S. Rutledge, "Higher Income and Uninsured: Common or Rare?" *Health Affairs* 26, no. 6 (2007): 1745–1752.

p. 71, "are now living without . . .": CBS, "Health Insurance for Young Adults," *CBS Early Show*, September 28, 2006.

p. 73, "approximately half of people . . .": "Health Care Costs Main Cause of Personal Bankruptcy, Study Finds," *NewStandard*, February 4, 2005, http://newstandardnews.net/content/?action=show_item&itemid=1439 (accessed November 6, 2008).

pp. 76–77, "requires hospital emergency departments . . .": James L. Thorne, "EMTALA: The Basic Requirements, Recent Court Interpretation: More HCFA Regulations to Come," American Academy of Emergency Medicine (Milwaukee, WI), http://www.aaem.org/emtala/watch.php (accessed March 4, 2008).

Chapter 5

p. 79, "reached $286.5 billion . . .": "U.S. Drug Sales in 2007 Grow at Slowest Rate Since 1961," *USA Today*, March 12, 2008.

p. 82, "In 1929 . . .": *JAMA*, 1999, 281 (1), 61–66.

p. 85, "They are one of the strongest . . .": Amy Allina, "Drugmakers Go Furthest to Sway Congress: 1,274 Lobbyists," *USA Today*, April 26, 2005.

p. 86, "1 in 5 teens has abused . . .": "Prescription Medicine Abuse: A Serious Problem," Partnership for a Drug-Free America, January 23, 2008.

p. 87, "out of it": Candice Ferrette, "'Robotripping' Grows Among Younger Teens," *Journal News*, April 21, 2008.

Chapter 6

p. 93, "while Americans value . . .": Barry Brown, "In Critical Condition: Health Care in America," *San Francisco Chronicle,* October 14, 2004.

p. 94, "Saskatchewan's 22-Month Wait . . .": Amy Jo Ehman, "Saskatchewan's 22-Month Wait for an MRI is 'Almost Criminal' Says Radiologists' Association," *Canadian Medical Association Journal,* March 2, 2004, http://www.cmaj.ca/cgi/content/full/170/5/776-a?maxtoshow=&HITS=10&hits=10 (accessed November 6, 2008).

p. 99, "as being in a crisis . . .": Sue Grant, "Healthcare in Germany," *MedHunters* magazine, July 19, 2004, http://www.medhunters.com/articles/healthcareInGermany.html (accessed March 7, 2008).

p. 99, "You may be interested . . .": George Trefgarne, "NHS reaches 1.4m employees," *Daily Telegraph,* March 22, 2005, http://www.telegraph.co.uk/finance/2912588/NHS-reaches-1.4m-employees.html (accessed March 23, 2005).

p. 105, "How is it possible . . .": Lisa McAdams, "Russia Readies Radical Health Care Reform," *Voice of America,* May 1, 2006, http://www.voanews.com/english/archive/2006-05/2006-05-01-voa31.cfm (accessed November 6, 2008).

Chapter 7

p. 106, "One of the great mysteries . . .": Malcolm Gladwell, "The Moral-Hazard Myth," *The New Yorker,* August 29, 2005, 2.

p. 109, "We face an impending crisis . . .": Randolph E. Schmid, "Medical Care System Not Ready for Mass of Aging Baby Boomers," *AARP Bulletin Today,* April 14, 2008, http://bulletin.aarp.org/yourhealth/policy/articles/medical_care_system_not_ready_for_mass_of_aging_baby_boomers_study_says1.html (accessed November 6, 2008).

pp. 114–115, "To replicate the FEHBP . . .": Aricka T. Flowers, "National Market Could Cure America's Health Care Crisis: Policy Analysts," *Heartland Institute,* January 1, 2007, http://www.heartland.org/Article.cfm?artId=20377 (accessed November 6, 2008).

p. 115, "I think one reason . . .": Flowers, "National Market Could Cure America's Health Care Crisis."

Further Information

Books

Canfield, Jack. *Chicken Soup for the Teenage Soul.* Deerfield Beach, FL: Health Communications, 2005.

Covey, Sean. *The Six Most Important Decisions You'll Ever Make: A Guide for Teens.* New York: Simon & Schuster, 2007.

Lawton, Sandra. *Sex Health Information for Teens.* Detroit: Omnigraphics, 2008.

Rose, Tracy. *Am I Fat? Factors and Prevention of Teen Obesity.* Lanham, MD: Rowman & Littlefield, 2007.

Volkmann, Chris. *From Binge to Blackout: A Mother and Son Struggle with Teen Drinking.* New York: NAL, 2006.

Websites

http://www.aap.org
From the American Academy of Pediatrics, covers health issues, including those of adolescents and young adults.

http://www.hhs.gov/children/index.shtml
Data from the Department of Health and Human Services on health topics from child abuse to teen problems.

http://www.KidsHealth.org
Fun and interactive stuff from health experts.

http://www.mypyramid.gov
Tips on maintaining a healthy weight and lifestyle.

Bibliography

Books

Angell, Marcia. *The Truth About the Drug Companies.*
New York: Random House, 2004.

Avorn, Jerry. *Powerful Medicines: The Benefits, Risks, and Costs of Prescription Drugs.* New York: Knopf, 2004.

Barlett, Donald L., and James B. Steele. *Critical Condition: How Health Care in America Became Big Business and Bad Medicine.* New York: Doubleday, 2004.

Critser, Greg. *Generation Rx: How Prescription Drugs Are Altering American Lives, Minds, and Bodies.* New York: Houghton Mifflin, 2005.

Farley, Tom, and Deborah A. Cohen. *Prescription for a Healthy Nation.* Boston: Beacon, 2005.

Greider, Katharine. *The Big Fix: How the Pharmaceutical Industry Rips off American Consumers.* Cambridge, MA: Perseus, 2003.

Halvorson, George. *Health Care Reform Now!* New York: Wiley, 2007.

LeBow, Robert H. *Health Care Meltdown: Confronting the Myths and Fixing Our Failing System.* Chambersburg, PA: Alan C. Hood, 2003.

Mahar, Maggie. *Money-Driven Medicine: The Real Reason Health Care Costs So Much.* New York: Collins, 2006.

Mechanic, David. *The Truth About Health Care.* New Brunswick, NJ: Rutgers University Press, 2006.

Richmond, Julius B., and Rashi Fein. *The Health Care Mess: How We Got Into It and What It Will Take to Get Out.* Cambridge, MA: Harvard University Press, 2005.

Rothman, Sheila M., and David J. Rothman. *The Pursuit of Perfection: The Promise and Peril Of Medical Enhancement.* New York: Pantheon, 2003.

Sered, Susan Starr, and Rushika Fernandopulle. *Uninsured in America.* Berkeley: University of California Press, 2005.

Articles

Kaiser Family Foundation and Health Research and Educational Trust. "Summary of Findings." Employer Health Benefits 2007 Annual Survey, September 11, 2007. http://www.kff.org/insurance/7672/upload/76723.pdf.

Kalogredis, Vasilios J. "Should You Consider Concierge Medicine?" *Physician's News Digest,* February 2004.

Kuttner, Hans, and Matthew S. Rutledge. "Higher Income and Uninsured: Common or Rare?" *Health Affairs,* 2007, 26(6):1745–1752.

Mishel, Lawrence. "Employers Shift Health Insurance Costs onto Workers." Economic Policy Institute, August 16, 2006. http://www.epi.org/content.cfm/webfeatures_snapshots_20060816 (accessed November 6, 2008).

National Cancer Institute. "Acute Lymphoblastic Leukemia in Children," National Cancer Institute Fact Sheet (July 11, 2002). http://www.cancer.gov/cancertopics/factsheet/ALLinchildren (accessed February 27, 2008).

National Coalition on Health Care. "Health Insurance Costs," National Coalition on Health Care, http://www.nchc.org/facts/cost.shtml (accessed November 6, 2008).

U.S. Department of Health and Human Services, Office of the Assistant Secretary for Planning and Evaluation. "Overview of the Uninsured in the United States: An Analysis of the 2005 Current Population Survey." Issue brief (September 22, 2005). http://aspe.hhs.gov/health/reports/05/uninsured-cps/index.htm (accessed February 7, 2008).

Index

Page numbers in **boldface** are illustrations, tables, and charts.

About the Author

A former U.S. Navy journalist and children's book editor, CORINNE J. NADEN lives in Tarrytown, New York. She is the author of more than one hundred nonfiction books for young readers. Her most recent book for Marshall Cavendish was *Political Campaigns* in our Open for Debate series.